Project Skills

TITLES IN THE

New Skills Portfolio series...

Series Editor: **Linda Holbeche**, Director of Research, Roffey Park Management Institute

Managing More with Less

Joanna Howard

Managing More with Less is an innovative book linking a range of core management skills and re-interpreting them to meet current organizational needs. Aimed at managers in flat organizations, this book shows you how to deal with increasingly scarce resources to maintain a high level of productivity.

0 7506 3698 X • paperback • May 1998

The Chameleon Manager

Brian Clegg

Today's managers are faced with many conflicting demands and situations. This book provides practical ways of achieving the impossible:

● How can you be a generalist and a specialist?
● How can you be an individual expert and a 'connected' team player?
● How can you manage more people with less time and fewer resources and be entrepreneurial at the same time?

Complete with its own website, http://www.cul.co.uk/chameleon, which gives further information and links to other sites.

0 7506 4026 X • paperback • June 1998

Project Skills

Sam Elbeik *and* Mark Thomas

Project Skills describes the best of the accepted project management techniques, taking the guesswork out of deciding which ones to apply at which stage. Elbeik and Thomas present a practical and accessible guide to managing projects of all sizes, not just large-scale ones.

0 7506 3978 4 • paperback • November 1998

Strategic Skills for Line Managers

Michael Colenso

Strategic Skills for Line Managers will help line managers and team leaders develop strategy at team or unit level. Increasingly, mid-level managers are required to think and act strategically and contribute extensively to strategy formulation.

0 7506 3982 2 • paperback • October 1998

Honing Your Knowledge Skills

Mariana Funes *and* Nancy Johnson

Honing Your Knowledge Skills looks at how to define knowledge working and identifies the practical skills of knowledge management needed by line managers. This book shows you how to:

● Handle information overload.
● Harness new ideas and become an expert.
● Turn knowledge into action.
● Understand IT resources and knowledge based systems.

0 7506 3699 8 • paperback • October 1998

Managing 'Live' Innovation

Michel Syrett *and* Jean Lammiman

Managing 'Live' Innovation examines the innovation process from the line manager's perspective. This book identifies the skills needed to manage live 'real time' innovation in an environment where products and services are constantly refined, and where customer input is encouraged from an early stage.

0 7506 3700 5 • paperback • November 1998

BUTTERWORTH HEINEMANN

Available from your local bookshop, or in case of difficulty call
Heinemann Customer Services on (01865) 888000

Project Skills

Sam Elbeik

Mark Thomas

OXFORD AUCKLAND BOSTON JOHANNESBURG MELBOURNE NEW DELHI

Butterworth-Heinemann
Linacre House, Jordan Hill, Oxford OX2 8DP
225 Wildwood Avenue, Woburn, MA 01801-2041
A division of Reed Educational and Professional Publishing Ltd

A member of the Reed Elsevier plc group

First published 1998

British Library Cataloguing in Publication Data
Elbeik, Sam
    Project skills. – (The new skills portfolio)
    1. Industrial project management
    I. Title   II. Thomas, Mark, 1958–
    658.4'04

ISBN 0 7506 3978 4

Typeset by Avocet Typeset, Brill, Aylesbury, Bucks
Printed and bound in Great Britain by Martins the Printers, Berwick Upon Tweed, Scotland

To Christine, my parents, Matt, Tarek and all my colleagues at IT Centre
Sam

To my late Father for his love, care and guidance
Mark

Contents

Series editor's preface

The last decade has seen considerable change in the world of employment. Organizations have shed roles and management layers in their attempt to be more cost-effective, competitive and closer to their customers. The 'leaner organization' concept, with its emphasis on teamworking, better use of technologies and greater opportunities for innovation, certainly appears to be benefiting many organizations which have seen improvements in quality and the bottom line. The trend towards ongoing organizational change and restructuring appears set to continue.

What appears to be successful as an organizational strategy may offer fewer benefits to employees however. Changing work practices have carried in their wake a degree of confusion. Job security cannot be taken for granted and ongoing hard work seems the order of the day. The dividing line between work and other aspects of life becomes increasingly blurred as mobile phones, e-mail, the Internet, remote conferencing means that employees are expected to be accessible anywhere, anytime. Teleworking, hot-desking and project working means that employees are expected to be largely self-managing, flexible and adaptable, able to work in teams which cross organizational boundaries and are in some cases virtual.

A key development in recent times is the increasing call for employees to manage their own careers, to think of themselves as self-employed, to upgrade their skills at the same time as holding down demanding jobs. The old 'psychological contract' by which employees might expect continuous employment and prospects of promotion up a vertical hierarchy in return for loyalty and effective performance, seems to have been replaced by the notion that employees can gain long-term security only by developing their skills and making themselves employable. Of course in the world of organized employment, there has been a buyers' market for jobs except in certain fields such as IT where limited supplies of skilled employees mean that it is the employees who hold the whip hand.

I have been carrying out research into the changing workplace, in particular the effect of flatter organization structures on careers, since 1994. This is very much in line with the mission of Roffey Park Management Institute, where I work, to investigate issues relating to the health and well-being of people at work. I have found that many people find the challenges of coping with ongoing change and constant hard work debilitating. Other people seem to have found the recipe for success and energy in this changing context. I have studied what appears to make some people cope so much more effectively with change than others do, and I have looked at some of the skills used by these individuals. It is the range of skills which enables these employees not only to survive but thrive in constantly changing organizations which is the focus of this series.

This series is intended to provide a self-help skills development resource. The authors have been selected not just because of their undoubted expertise in the subject matter of their book, but also because they can write in a way which will enable you to develop or enhance your ability in the skill in question. This is not 'just a lot of theory'. Rather, each book offers a blend of practical activities, background information and examples from organizations and individuals, which should make sense whether you are simply dipping in for the odd idea, or working through in a systematic way. The books offer a range of insights and suggestions for further learning which will be useful to the serious self-developer. They focus on the truly transferable 'meta-skills' of lifelong learning.

So whether you are a specialist who recognizes the need to develop a broader business understanding, or a generalist who sees the need to develop some real 'knowledge' skills, this series has something to offer. Books in the series address some of the key skill areas for current and future success. Based on my research, I propose that the ability to think and act strategically is vital at any level in an organization. New approaches to thinking creatively and introducing innovation will become increasingly important, as will the ability to work in a range of different types of team. Project working is becoming commonplace and the 'new' project skills are as relevant to team members as to team leaders. As the workplace continues to evolve, the ability to work effectively in a range of networks and informal groupings will be valuable.

Above all, the people who acquire the ability to manage themselves and their time, including taking responsibility for their own career, are likely to be the people who can exercise genuine choice. Knowing what you want, developing your skills and having the ability to make things happen is likely to make you truly employable. As some organizations have already found to their cost, employees whose skills are in demand are able to make their own choices rather than having to rely on their employer. Perhaps making a commitment to yourself and your development is the surest guarantee of securing what is important to you. Good luck and enjoy the journey!

Linda Holbeche
Director of Research
Roffey Park Management Institute

Acknowledgements

In writing this book we wanted to add quotes from people working in a variety of organizations who had several years of experience running projects. We were moved by the willingness of these people who kindly gave up their time to share their experience and advice with us. We feel that their quotes have kept us focused on the writing about the practical aspects of managing projects.

We would like to thank the following: Dalim Basu, Project Manager, ITN; Gregoire Bouille, MIS Analyst – Methodology and Education, Philip Morris; Flavio De Rosa, Clinical Scientist, F Hoffman La Roche; Howard Gerlis, MBCS, Member of Council, British Computer Society; Alan Goodson, Project Leader, The Dow Chemical Company; Paul L'Estrange, Manager – Development Support, Philip Morris; Dennis O'Gorman, Senior Project Manager, Fitzpatrick Contractors; Phillip Obraztsov, Regional Manager, Microsoft; Andreas Schmidt, Business Information Manager, Novartis; Peter Suhr-Jessen, Project Manager, Novo Nordisk; Gabriel Williams RIBA, Managing Partner, Petersen Williams Architects.

1 Real-world project management

Why is this book different?

The subject of project management has developed over the years into a fairly precise set of techniques, definitions and practices that are applicable to running projects. Full-time project managers with a number of years of experience understand these practices and endeavour to apply them when managing their projects. Unfortunately, many projects are managed by people who have been thrust into the project management role as well as continuing with their day-to-day activities. After being sent on a project management course by their organization, the expectation is that they can deliver the project objectives with their newly gained knowledge. It is not surprising that several recent surveys conclude that up to 80 per cent of projects are delivered late and are over budget.

The secret to successful project management practice is knowing when to apply the appropriate technique at the right stage in a project. The Project Management Institute Standards Committee, USA, identify this by saying:

The knowledge and practices (of project management) ... are applicable to most projects most of the time ... [it] does not mean that the knowledge and practices described are or should be applied uniformly on all projects. (Project Management Institute Standards Committee, *A Guide to the Project Management Body of Knowledge*)

All too often for the first few times when someone is asked to manage a project they will try to apply all the techniques they have been taught, thinking that if a particular technique is omitted, the project will fail. They soon find out that they do not have the time to apply all the techniques and begin to drop one after the other.

This book describes accepted project management techniques, but we have selected only the most essential techniques, which takes the guesswork out of deciding which ones to apply at which stage. It also presents 'people' skills essential to making a project succeed. These skills include team-building, leadership and motivating others to deliver.

People make the project team

Try not to lose your head, even when all around you seem to be losing theirs. Stay calm. Try anyway – then if you need to shout, go and have a good scream in a room on your own! (Dalim Basu, Project Manager, ITN)

All projects need a number of different people to make them happen, and to make them succeed. This book is aimed primarily at the person who has to manage the project, although all practising managers will benefit from the fundamental techniques that are presented.

Simply understanding the need for the involvement of a number of groups (Figure 1.1) is in itself a benefit in making a project succeed.

Project managers

New project managers who have not experienced the development of a project, as well as seasoned project managers, will benefit from

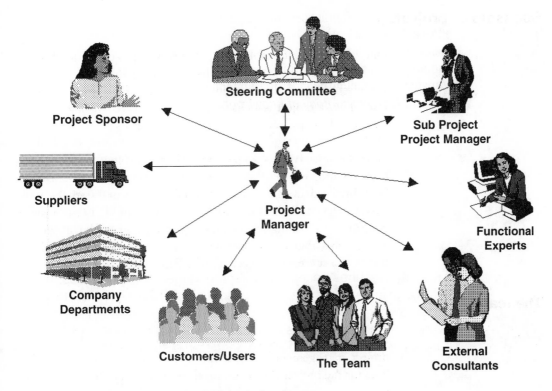

Figure 1.1 Who does the project manager deal with?

the techniques described in this book. One of the main lessons to emerge is that project management is not about using the latest software to produce impressive-looking charts that are displayed on a wall for all to see at the office. Rather, it is more about understanding and using the variety of tools and techniques that are available. Indeed, many of these only require minimal use of computers. The critical skill is focusing people's thoughts on to a problem in a structured way.

Most project managers are traditionally taught to develop a detailed project plan of all the activities needed to complete the project. This approach is not always appropriate in a world where rapid changes in technology can significantly change the details of a plan. In most cases, only an outline plan is required of the main project activities, followed by the traditional detail of the first-stage activities. Understanding this critical point can save many hours of needless effort in initially recording all the activities involved, only to have to change them a few weeks later.

Sponsors of projects

One of the biggest problems for sponsors of projects is to visualize the whole picture when it comes to commissioning a project. Understanding all the different elements necessary to successfully implement a project is a challenging task, and recognizing the need for each of these elements will give them a head start.

Have the objectives been agreed with the team? How often will feedback on progress be given? Have all the appropriate departments been involved from the start? Should internal or external people resources be used? The questions are almost endless, but the answers contribute to making up the bigger picture. This book will provide a framework that any project sponsor can use to ensure that all elements of a successful project actually happen.

The team

For a project to succeed the team should recognize the need for project management; what it means and what their contribution does for the project. The team needs to understand the key stages of managing a project and the impact of their work on the whole project. Individuals make up a team and recognizing the efforts of the project manager in building, leading and motivating the team is vital to the success of the project.

Functional experts and advisers

Functional experts such as members of a Human Resource Department, Finance Department or Marketing Department often participate in projects because they are the recipients of a system or process, or their areas provide the rules for developing systems or processes. But such people cannot act in isolation. Participating fully at the beginning as well as during the life of a project is critical for it to succeed. Understanding the roles of other participants as well as their own role contributes to eventual success. A project that progresses without regular checks, or feedback, from such functional experts during development often results in failure.

Leading and motivating the team

Understanding what motivates people will help us explain and manage their behaviour, thus allowing the team leader to get the most out of team members. Any project manager is expected to have team-leading qualities and be capable of motivating other people.

Understanding that a wide variety of people contribute to the project team, from the sponsor to the functional expert, is an essential element in successful project management. Time and effort must therefore be spent on understanding what motivates each person or group. In turn, appropriate management action must follow.

The project manager who is a team leader must strike a balance between implementing the tools and techniques as well as applying appropriate people management skills. Asking a science technician to keep to strict time schedules when analysing blood samples may be necessary to keep a bio-research project within budget, but providing a clear sense of direction by reminding the technician of the end goals is vital.

Project team structures

There are a number of ways organizations are structured to cope with day-to-day business. Classical structures include hierarchical, product and matrix and in many cases, a single organization may well have a mixture of these structures. Modern communication facilities such as video conferencing and the Internet have also made possible the virtual organization.

The essence of a project team is that it brings together individuals from within an organization and from external suppliers who are highly focused on completing project deliverables to support a project objective.

Functional organizations

The functional organization (Figure 1.2) is characterized by a rigid structure of reporting lines and is often described as a pyramid, with

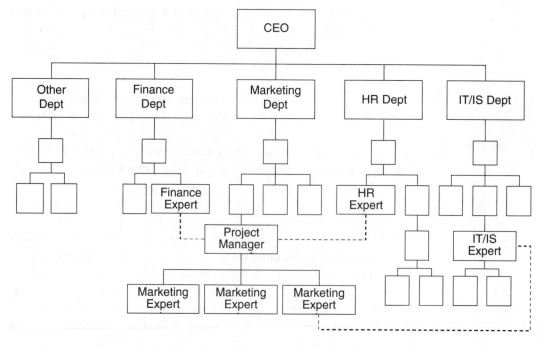

Figure 1.2 The functional organization

power residing at the top of the pyramid. The executive at the top of such organizations, the chief executive officer (CEO), will have a number of managers reporting to him or her. These managers will typically head departments or functions such as Information Technology (IT or IS), Human Resource (HR), Marketing, Production, Finance, and Research and Development (R&D).

Projects are carried out in each department where most of the project team comprises individuals from within the department. A number of functional experts from other departments will also work on the project, but they will work from within their own departments and are usually physically separated from the majority of the project team. There will be a project leader, again coming from within the department, who would report to the head of department.

Advantages

● The majority of the functional specialists easily share their knowledge because they come from the same department and normally work together.

- It is easier to implement work rules and regulations for a group of similar functional experts.
- They will also share a commonality of perspective that will help the main thrust of a project.

Disadvantages

- Responses to change in market conditions are usually slow. These take time to implement because requests for approval have to be sought through several functional management chains.
- Communicating and co-ordinating the team is difficult because team members are split across several functional departments within the organization.
- Rivalries and conflicts may result.

Product organizations

The product organization (Figure 1.3) arranges its functional experts within teams that work towards delivering a new product. Much of the authority for approval rests with the product manager and so

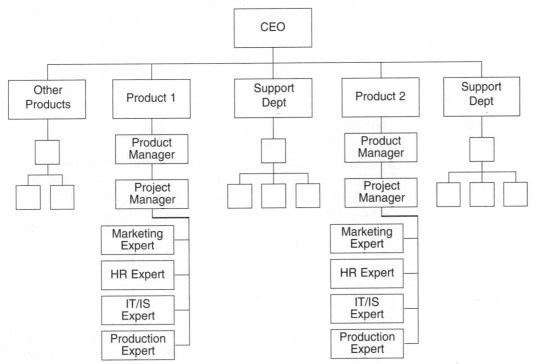

Figure 1.3 The product organization

there is a shorter chain of command to the overall organization manager.

Advantages

- Reaction to market changes is rapid as authority exists in the project team.
- All team members, who are functional specialists work for the same project leader.

Disadvantages

- Duplication of functional experts will exist across the organization as they are each dedicated to a single project.
- There is a lack of information exchange between functional experts as they are located in different parts of the organization.

Matrix organizations

The matrix-based organization (Figure 1.4) is characterized by having a pool of project managers who will be assigned to projects

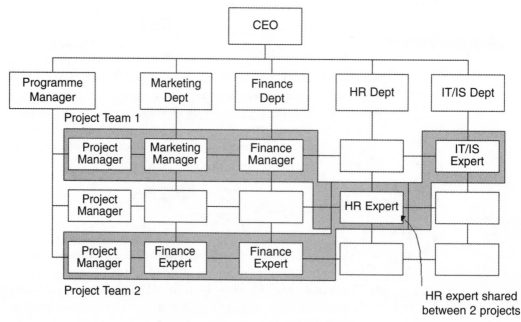

Figure 1.4 The matrix organization

as they are commissioned. The functional experts are provided by departmental line managers until the project ends. The experts then return to their respective departments and report to their line managers.

Advantages

- Response to changing project needs is very rapid.
- Functional experts are more part of a team and are more focused on project deliverables.
- Team members have a functional department to return to after the project.
- Their respective departments look after their careers and specific development needs.

Disadvantages

- There can be conflict between functional line managers and project managers over the deployment of resource.
- If the team is not physically located in the same area in a building, communications and control becomes a difficulty.
- Matrix structures are frequently hindered by accusations of poor accountability and lack of clarity in responsibilities.

Virtual organizations

Virtual organizations (Figure 1.5) are real and are here today. These organizations usually have a small physical presence, typically a head office, and the functional experts work from client locations or their homes. They rarely travel to the organization's offices and rely heavily on personal computers and communication devices such as telephone, fax, e-mail and video conferencing.

Advantages

- The organization maintains reduced financial overheads, as there is no requirement to maintain office space for all employees.
- Procedural standards must be enforced to maintain quality and control of project deliverables, as team members do not work at a single location.

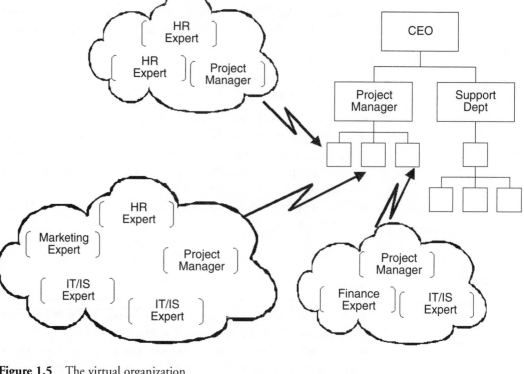

Figure 1.5 The virtual organization

Disadvantages

- More effort must be put into motivating the individual team members because they tend to work in isolation and lose social contact with other members of the team.

Small project structures

Irrespective of how an organization structures its projects, it is generally accepted that every project must have, as a minimum, a project sponsor and a project manager. The sponsor commissions the project and the project manager defines, plans and controls the project as well as carrying out the actual tasks. There is a danger that, even on a small project, the project manager spends most of his or her time on the actual tasks, and does not spend enough time on managing the project. Typical consequences of this are that the project end date slips, or the quality of the deliverables is compromised.

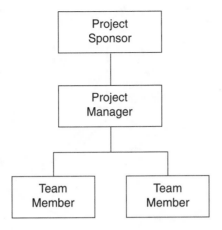

Figure 1.6 Project structure for smaller projects

A project manager running a small project must continually assess whether he or she has the time to carry out the project tasks as well as manage the project. Quite often some of the work can be delegated to other people, or experts, in the organization, giving the project manager more time to manage the project. These experts need to be managed and, although they do not formally report to the project manager from an organizational point of view, they are part of the project team and are responsible for working on project tasks.

A typical project structure for smaller projects is shown in Figure 1.6.

Larger project structures

On larger projects, the number of people involved can increase significantly. Figure 1.7 shows the various relationships, roles and structure.

Roles and responsibilities

On reviewing the previous sections, it is clear that a variety of skilled people are involved in running projects. We have looked at different organizational structures and at small and large project structures.

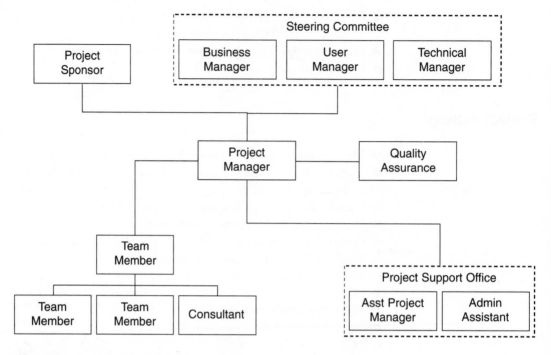

Figure 1.7 Project structure for larger projects

We now summarize the roles and responsibilities of the people involved in delivering a project.

Project sponsor

- Commissions and owns the project.
- Is clear about the objectives and scope.
- Finds and wins resource(s) for the project.
- Chairs the steering committee.
- Is enthusiastic about the project.
- Represents the first-line issue resolution for the project manager.

Steering committee

- Project sponsor creates the steering committee.
- Has representatives from business and technical functions and user community.
- Reviews overall project direction, schedule, costs and quality of deliverables.

- Resolves major issues/problems.
- Sponsor chairs the steering committee.
- Project manager attends steering committee meetings.
- Typically meets every few weeks.

Project manager

- Manages the project, the people and paperwork.
- Responsible for achieving project objectives within scope, time and budget.
- Prepares the Terms of Reference, and plans the baseline.
- Evaluates risk and prepares contingency.
- Controls the project and implements the plan.
- Builds, leads and motivates the team.
- Reviews and replans.
- Maintains good communications with team and all stakeholders.
- Makes regular presentations.
- Tackles problem areas sooner rather than later.
- Manages sponsor expectations.

Team member

- Technical expert qualified to complete project tasks.
- Gives regular feedback on progress to project manager.
- Focuses on delivering quality.
- Contributes to teamwork and moral.

Project support office

- Created on large projects.
- Provides administrative support to project manager and team.
- Collects time sheets.
- Prepares progress reports and meeting minutes.
- Updates project plan with tracking information.
- Responsible for project accounting.

Quality assurance

- Carries out project quality reviews.
- Is not part of the project team.
- Is an independent person giving unbiased opinions.

Essential project activities

This introduction focuses on two key points:

1 People, and teams, make a project succeed
2 The essential project stages.

The critical things that are needed to run a successful
project are:
● Focus
● Commitment
● The ability and authority to make decisions. (Phillip Obraztsov, Regional
Manager, Microsoft)

In summary, a project can be divided into six distinct stages. These
make up the classic project management model (Figure 1.8):

1 Define.
2 Plan.
3 Team-building, leading and motivation.
4 Control.
5 Communications.
6 Review.

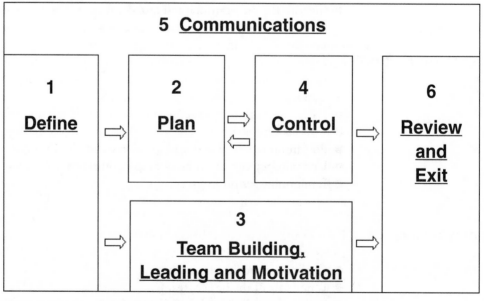

Figure 1.8 Classic six-stage project management model

In the *define* stage, the project manager prepares a document that records the essential client requirements that describes, at a minimum, what the project objectives are. The document also covers what the deliverables will be and when these will be delivered, together with an estimate of the project costs.

In the second stage, a project *plan* is prepared which describes in more detail the project tasks, their dependencies, schedules, resources needed, more detailed costs and a risk analysis to determine any contingency needs.

As the plan is being prepared, the third stage also begins. This is where the *team* is identified. They also quite often become involved in the planning of the project. These team members are the experts who will carry out the project. Their technical experience is a great benefit at this stage, especially when estimating the duration and dependencies of tasks. This third stage continues throughout the life of the project, where the project manager has to *lead* and continually *motivate* the team and individuals.

During the *control* stage, the plan is implemented and the team carry out the tasks needed to meet the project objectives. Reviews are held to track actual progress against the original plan. Regular reviews and adjustments of the plan are carried out to keep the team focused on the project deliverables.

Communications, the fifth stage of our approach, is carried out throughout the project and is essential for success. Memos are circulated, formal reports and presentations are made almost on a continual basis. Informal communications; conversations between colleagues outside the team environment, are also important as they allow the project manager to keep a close track of what is really going on.

The *review* stage is the last stage in our six-part project management model. Information is gathered to assess the effectiveness of the project manager and the project process. The aim is to record and learn important lessons from the project so that these can be used or avoided in the next project.

Each of these stages will be discussed in more detail in subsequent chapters.

2 Understanding projects

What is a project?

A project is a collection of tasks that is carried out by a team to meet an objective as defined by a sponsor. It has a beginning and end date, a budget, and risk. No two projects are ever the same.

Consider work that you are currently doing and ask yourself the following questions:

- *Are there clear, measurable and attainable objectives?*
- *Have the work tasks been identified?*
- *Do you know who will be carrying out these tasks?*
- *Who is the sponsor of the work?*
- *Do you have a great team to execute the project?*
- *Do you know when the work needs to begin?*
- *When will all the work be finished?*
- *Have funds been set aside to pay for this work?*
- *Are you unsure that the right work has been identified?*
- *Have the risks been identified and a contingency documented?*

If the answer to any of these questions is 'no', then you either do not have a project or have overlooked a significant component of a project. For example:

- Negotiations between two industrial groups who have a dispute over working conditions may never find a resolution. A common objective may not be defined or agreed, and an end date for settling the dispute may not be defined or attainable. This is not a project, this is a dispute.
- A production line producing bottled soft drinks does not have an end date for finishing production. This is a process not a project.
- Designing, building and commissioning a soft drinks production line has all the elements of a project. This is a project.
- A computer software developer who spends time building a customer contact system for their department in their spare time has no sponsor. This is not a project, this is an initiative.

It can be argued that for some projects, the 'team' can be just one person, but in most cases effort is needed by a number of different people. For example, a project usually has a team which involves suppliers, other department members, end users, technical specialists and temporary staff.

Three main project dimensions

All projects can be described as having the following three dimensions:

- budget
- schedule
- quality of deliverables.

All three dimensions are interlinked (Figure 2.1). If, for example, the schedule needs to change to create an earlier end date for the project, then quite often the budget needs to increase and the number of deliverables will reduce to maintain quality.

A good discipline at the beginning of any project is to understand people's views on the importance of the balance, or mix, of these three dimensions.

Budget

Schedule

Balance

Quality of Deliverables

Figure 2.1   The priority of three main project dimensions often upsets the balance required

Consider the different views and perspectives of the importance of the three dimensions – budget, schedule and quality of deliverables. Ask yourself if all three dimensions are equally important to each of the following people or groups, or is one of the dimensions more important than the others:

○ *the sponsor*
○ *the functional expert*
○ *the line manager*
○ *the supplier or contractor*
○ *the customer or end user*
○ *the project manager.*

Record your answers in Figure 2.2 and compare them with the following comments.

Which three project dimensions of Budget ($), Schedule (t) and Quality of Deliverables (Q) do these people focus on?

	$	t	Q
Sponsor			
Functional Expert			
Line Manager			
Supplier or Contractor			
Customer or End User			
Project Manager			

Figure 2.2 Key project dimensions: where should the focus of the team effort be?

The sponsor

The sponsor often focuses first on the budget and then on the schedule. During later stages he or she may focus more sharply on the quality of the deliverables. At the beginning of a project, the sponsor will often ask the following:

● How much is it costing?
● How can I reduce project spending?
● Do I really need to spend on this additional resource?
● Can we meet our schedule without additional spending?
● Do we really need to deliver this?

Towards the end of a project, the sponsor's focus will change and he or she will often ask:

● Why hasn't this been done?
● Do you think the customer will accept this?
● The quality of this is not good enough.
● How are we supposed to market this?

The functional expert

The functional expert forms the core of the development team and is primarily focused on the quality of their work. He or she will also focus on the scheduling aspect of the project as this will impact on other work already scheduled.

The line manager

The line manager is not directly involved in the project, but provides from his or her team the functional experts as a resource. The manager's concern is to find out when this resource will return to his or her own team, so the manager's interest in the project is primarily to do with the schedule. If you need additional resource, you often have to clear this with a line manager.

The supplier or contractor

Although suppliers or contractors involved in a project should balance all three project dimensions, they often focus on the budget and schedule first and then on the quality of the deliverables. They will first consider how much income they would receive from the project and how much of their time is demanded by the schedule.

Customers or end users

The customers or end users often look at the time dimension first. When will they receive the project deliverable? After they receive the output of the project, they then consider the quality.

The project manager

The project manager has to focus continually on all three of the project dimensions – budget, schedule and quality of deliverables. Recognizing that different people have different priorities for these three dimensions is important, because more emphasis is placed on one or more of them at appropriate times.

A simple but effective technique to use when a person places too much emphasis on one of these dimensions is to highlight the dependency on the other two dimensions. For example, if a sponsor asks for the schedule to be reduced, show the relationship between the three dimensions and ask the sponsor to support the request by providing more funds and resources.

Rapid change governs how projects are managed

Be prepared for surprises, changes, improvements but don't lose focus. (Peter Suhr-Jessen, Project Manager, Novo Nordisk)

One of the main difficulties in mastering the management of projects is knowing how much time to spend on a particular activity such as obtaining requirements, documenting the project scope, working and motivating the team or gathering time sheets as part of the control process.

In order to answer this question it is important to understand which market sector the project is operating in with respect to change. Two types of change should be considered. Technology change and requirements change. Figure 2.3 plots four different market sectors in relation to changing technology and project requirements.

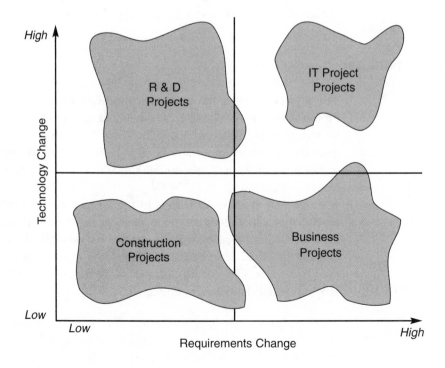

Figure 2.3 Change affecting different market sectors

NEW SKILLS PORTFOLIO

Understand the market sector you are operating in and identify the type of change you will face:

- Rapid change in technology – speed to market is probably all that a project manager can use as a tool to combat the high rate of technological change.
- Changing requirements – understanding and adapting a project management methodology will provide a framework to manage changing requirements.

Construction projects

Construction projects tend to operate in a relatively stable environment with respect to changing technology and changing requirements. Implementation of advances in construction techniques occurs during several years. For example, concrete technology has not changed radically over the last decade. Project requirements are usually fairly straightforward: a bridge needs to be built between two points, or a building needs to be constructed for office purposes. Managing such projects, while demanding, is not normally affected by constant change.

Business projects

Business projects are often affected by changing project requirements. These are often the result of changes in project sponsor, mergers and acquisitions, or changes in business practices. A project looking at a new management structure within an organization can easily have its objectives changed as a result of a merger with another organization. Suddenly the objectives may be to review two different management structures and to recommend a new unified one. A change of sponsor often impacts the objectives of a business project. The sponsor's business experience will be brought to the project and will often result in changes to the project. These changes make managing business projects difficult.

Research and development projects

These projects often have long-term objectives that do not often change. For example, in the pharmaceutical industry, the objective of an R&D project to find a compound of vaccine to treat a particular illness, may be unchanged for many years. In the automobile industry, the project objective to develop a concept car may also remain the same for several years. However, the changes in technology that is available to these and other industries during an R&D project will often affect the way the project is managed. Although the objective many not change, the scope, resources and timescale often will.

Information technology projects

With IT or IS projects, changes in technology and project requirements happen with such frequency that even recording these changes becomes a major task and often contributes to project failure. Another example is where computer software, developed to run under a particular operating system, may not necessarily run under the next release of that operating system. Such software development projects have to be completed rapidly in order to achieve a respectable return on investment, or simply to be usable before being redundant.

Key to successful projects

'Dilbert' is not fiction and generally understates the case (you wouldn't believe how true to life Dilbert is)! (Flavio De Rosa, Clinical Scientist, F. Hoffman La Roche)

Looking at several reviews on project statistics over the last few years, constant and worrying messages are presented. Some of these are listed below.

On most projects:

● The team is not sure of the project objectives.
● The team is not sure what the project deliverables are.
● At the end of the project, the objectives are only partially met.
● The planned schedule often runs late.
● The budget is often exceeded.
● The use of computer automation assists in planning but is not used for control.

On a sizeable minority of projects:

Rank	Success Factors
1	Clearly defined objectives
2	Good planning and control method
3	Good quality of project manager
4	Good management support
5	Enough time and resource
6	Commitment by all
7	High user involvement
8	Good communications
9	Good project organization and structure
10	Being able to stop a project

Figure 2.4 Typically what people from global organizations see as critical for the success of a project

- The project fails.
- The project is abandoned.
- Users' training needs are not addressed.
- Users are not consulted on their requirements.

If you asked a variety of people from a global organization to identify and rank those factors which are key to the success of their projects, you would typically get the response shown in Figure 2.4.

What is interesting from these results is that most project managers and project team members understand the need for clearly defined objectives and having a good planning and control method. So why is it that most projects fail to meet their objectives, have ill-defined deliverables, run behind schedule and are often over budget? Perhaps it is a lack of discipline on the part of the project manager and team members to implement their project management methodology. It is probably more true to say that inexperienced project managers believe all elements of a project management methodology have to be implemented, which requires a great deal of time and energy. After a few months, the benefits of a project management methodology are not clear and are seen, in many cases, as an overhead and unnecessary burden. Available time to the project manager is further eroded as in many cases, a dedicated project manager is not allocated full time to a project, but also has to carry out his or her 'other' specialist day job, for example, in marketing, systems analysis or as a human resource specialist.

The immense time pressure on the project manager results in significant parts of a project methodology being ignored. As a result, there is a high probability that the project fails to meet its objectives.

This book advocates and describes a methodology that requires a highly efficient but minimum amount of effort to plan and control a project; including the maintenance of good communications, team-building and leadership activities.

Main stages and activities of any project

As introduced in the previous chapter, our classic project management model can be divided into the following six distinct stages:

1 define
2 plan
3 team-building, leading and motivation
4 control
5 communications
6 review.

Figure 2.5 presents these six stages, their relationship from start to finish and the outputs generated during each stage.

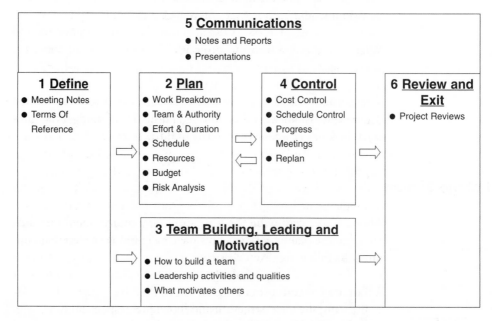

Figure 2.5 Essential stages in classic six-stage project management model and their outputs

In summary, after the define stage (stage 1), the detailed plan is created in stage 2 and the team is identified in stage 3. Once the plan has been approved, the project is implemented by the team and the control stage (stage 4) is started. Stage 3, Team-building, leading and motivation still continues as team members are assigned to tasks and the project manager continues to motivate individuals and develop the efficiency of the team. At the end of the control stage, stage 4, the project deliverables are completed and the project comes to an end. Unless another project requires the services of the existing team, the team is disbanded and a project review is carried out in stage 6, review and exit. The communications stage (stage 5), is conducted throughout the entire duration of the project. The following sections describe each of these stages in more detail.

Project stage 1: define

Defining the client requirements is the first stage in a project. This is a fundamental process that requires a significant amount of time and effort to clarify. The main aim of this stage is to:

- Define the project objectives in a document called the 'Terms of Reference' (TOR).
- Start to build a good relationship with the sponsor.

The TOR is a document that records the project objectives, scope, constraints, assumptions (at this stage), deliverables, dates and an estimate of costs. Unless TORs are created and then signed off and agreed by the sponsor, the project will most likely fail from the beginning.

The outputs of this stage are meeting notes, that have been created during discussions with the sponsor, and the TOR which is the 'contract' between the project manager and the sponsor.

Project stage 2: plan

About 15 per cent of all the time spent on a project should be dedicated to the planning stage. This stage will produce a plan that contains the following seven elements:

1 Creating a work breakdown structure (WBS).
2 Creating the team structure and individual responsibilities.
3 Estimating effort and duration for each task.

4 Preparing the schedule.
5 Allocating resource to tasks.
6 Determining the budget.
7 Risk analysis and contingency.

The WBS is a chart showing the relationship of all major tasks. From the WBS emerges the team structure and individual responsibilities. The effort and duration has to be estimated for each task and the resource allocated to the tasks. The schedule for all tasks is then drawn up which shows the start and end date for the project and a budget is prepared. Finally a risk analysis is carried out which shows any contingency required.

All these activities make up the plan that is subsequently reviewed and agreed by the sponsor. The plan now forms a baseline for the project where progress can be measured and controlled.

Project stage 3: team-building, leading and motivation

Team-building activity

Managing people in a newly formed team in the most part involves a complex set of drives and emotions such as ambition, motivation, competition, power, control, co-operation, trust and mistrust. No project can be managed without the need to manage relationships, which is often the most demanding aspect of project management. Team-building is all about managing the various group dynamics which include the interplay of roles, skills, expertise and relationships between various team members and other interested parties.

Leading

The project manager has to provide a clear sense of direction and display a great deal of energy to push for results. He or she also needs to delegate work and avoid doing everything him or herself. The project manager must be available to the team and fight for their needs as well as being able to make tough decisions and say 'no'. Finally, as a leader, the project manager must create an environment of mutual trust and manage the politics that may frequently surround some projects.

Motivation activity

Motivation is the engine that makes a team member commit to do specific things. This commitment comes from within the individual.

If a team member has decided not to do something there is very little any project manager can do. The opposite is also true. Part of the project manager's responsibilities is to understand what motivates the team members, which will help to explain and predict their behaviour. The project manager must create the right atmosphere and environment to cause people to work together to achieve a common goal.

Project stage 4: control

This is the part of a project where most of the effort is spent, where the tasks are carried out by the team as defined in the plan. To maintain control of the project, the project manager needs to hold regular progress meetings with the team, sponsor, steering committee, suppliers, end users, departmental line managers and sub-project managers. This is a busy time and regular reports need to be produced by the project office and communicated to a variety of people, mainly the sponsor, steering committee and team. These reports include progress to date including schedule controls, change requests, budget controls and a replan if required.

In addition to holding regular progress meetings, a process must be put in place to control change. Quite often, this change process does not exist and changes are implemented without considering the impact on the plan.

At the end of this stage the projected deliverables are presented and there will be period of testing by the customer or end users.

Project stage 5: communications

Don't underestimate the value of marketing your project to everyone. (Paul L'Estrange, Manager – Development Support, Philip Morris)

Communication occurs throughout the life of any project. From the initial meeting with the client, verbal and written communications are carried out endlessly. At each of the six stages during the project, a number of documents are produced, and these need to be written and circulated to an agreed list of people. Formal presentations will also have to be made. The aim is to avoid surprises and manage expectations of all parties by advising on progress and problem areas at all times.

Project stage 6: review

The review stage of a project is usually carried out by the quality assurance manager who wants to determine the effectiveness of:

● the project manager and team
● the project process.

At the end of the review a document is prepared and presented to the sponsor and project manager by the quality assurance manager. A meeting is then held to discuss the review and some action points may arise. Several important lessons can be learnt, particularly what to avoid doing in the next project. The project is now finished.

3 Project stage 1: define

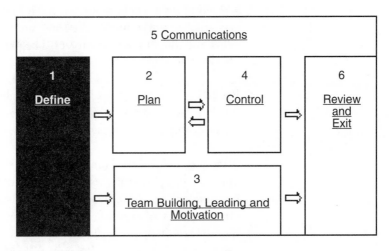

Figure 3.1   Define

Sometimes it feels like you are trying to please all of the people all of the time. Therefore it is critical to manage the customer's expectations from the very start. Never promise something you cannot deliver. (Howard Gerlis MBCS, Member of Council, British Computer Society)

Clearly understanding and documenting the sponsor's requirements is the first stage in defining a project. This is a fundamental process that requires a significant amount of time from the project manager to get it right. By understanding your sponsor's requirements you will be identifying the project objectives and scope. You are trying to answer the questions:

- What is this project all about (the objectives and scope)?
- What does the sponsor want from this project (the deliverables)?
- When does the sponsor want the deliverables?
- When will this project end?
- What will the cost be?
- Who will be involved?

One of the greatest problems for new project managers is understanding that the answers to these questions, especially the project objectives, are very rarely documented, and are quite often unclear at the beginning of a project. In most cases, the sponsor will believe that he or she has clear project objectives and has clearly communicated this to the project manager. Communication of these objectives may often be in a memo form, but is also often given verbally, and the project manager may not even realize that this has taken place. The project manager has to develop skills that alert them when a project has just been commissioned and to develop a list of questions to clarify client requirements.

Requests to manage a project come by phone, at meetings, over a lunch or even at social or sporting events outside work hours. Project managers have to be prepared.

After the initial alert from the sponsor that a project has started, understanding his or her requirements and project objectives usually means attending a meeting to discuss and clarify these further. Quite often a series of meetings is needed to finally agree what your sponsor requirements really are, and these are recorded in a document called the 'Terms of Reference'.

The main aims of the define stage are to begin:

- building a good sponsor relationship
- recording project objectives in the TOR.

Building a good sponsor relationship

Three fundamental rules of project management success are the client, the client and the client. (Gabriel Williams RIBA, Managing Partner, Petersen Williams Architects)

The first few meetings when the project manager is gathering the sponsor's requirements for the project are early opportunities to build a good sponsor relationship. Asking the right questions is vital to gain the information to define the project. First we will examine what sort of questions we should be asking at meetings followed by good meeting etiquette.

Asking the right questions at meetings to build good relationships

Your initial meeting is often the most important because your sponsor will have greater tolerance when being asked fundamental questions. So get your basic questions in early. Remember, you are trying to build a good relationship with your sponsor, so you need to ask questions that may not immediately be relevant to the project. It may help to go into the meeting with a form that prompts you to ask the appropriate question. For this, the sponsor meeting form (Figure 9.2 in Chapter 9) will prove useful.

At the initial meeting you need to:

● Confirm the purpose of your meeting.
● Learn about the sponsor and his or her operation.
● Begin building sponsor relationship.
● Understand sponsor problems and issues.
● Begin to define clear project objectives and scope.
● Explain your project methodology.
● Agree next steps.
● Use the project definition – sponsor meeting form.

Note down some questions you could ask in order to obtain the above information.

Here are a few questions that you could use to begin collecting information.

Confirm the purpose of your meeting

You should get the response to this question early on if you do not have an agenda prepared or agreed beforehand.

● I have prepared an agenda for this meeting, does this look OK?

● I understand we are here to talk about ... Is this true?
● Is half an hour sufficient time to talk about ... ?

Learn about the sponsor and his or her operation

In many cases a sponsor will tell you about his or her operation and your difficulty may be to stop them talking about this one point and move them on to the next subject. Allow them to talk and take a genuine interest in what he or she says. Do not try to hurry them, but you can pick an appropriate moment to change the topic by using a sentence like 'So, your operation is about ... Do you have a clear view about the objectives for this project?'. If he or she have not told you already, try one of the following questions to find out what the operation is all about:

● Can you give me the background to your operation?
● Can you tell me what your department does?
● How does your operation fit into the rest of the organization?

Begin building sponsor relationship

One of your main objectives at the beginning of a project is to begin building a business relationship with the sponsor. Gaining an insight into other business or personal aspects of the sponsor will begin to create a good working bond. Looking around the office you may see something that you can ask questions on:

● I see you are interested in ...
● How long have you been a member of ...
● What a great view, how long have you worked from this office?

Understand sponsor problems and issues

Although you are trying to understand the objectives of the project, allowing your sponsor to talk about other problems or issues may give you a better insight into why this project is being commissioned. Showing an interest in other issues your sponsor raises also helps to build a good business relationship:

● What do you see as your problem areas?
● Are there any other issues related to this project that we should discuss?
● Will this project impact on other areas of the business?

Begin to define clear project objectives and scope

This is the most important part of the meeting with your sponsor as you are trying to determine what the project objectives are and what is within and outside of the scope for the project. Writing down and discussing the project objectives often leads to a stage where the sponsor realizes that he or she are not clear about the objectives, or that a number of objectives exist leading to more than one project being commissioned. Here are some of the questions you need to ask to clarify what the objectives and scope for the project are:

- What are the project objectives?
- Why is this project being done?
- What will this project deliver?
- Are you the sponsor of this project?
- When should the project finish?
- Is there a budget for this work?
- Will any special equipment be needed?
- Will we need anybody with specialist knowledge?
- Who else will be involved?
- Are there any departments that will not be involved?
- Has the team been identified?
- Is there a steering committee?

Explain your project methodology

It is always good practice to let your sponsor know the project methodology you intend to use. Outline your six stages, explaining that you are currently at stage 1, define. Let them know that you will be submitting a detailed plan during stage 2, plan, and that you will begin to mobilize and build the team in stage 3. You will lead and motivate the team as you continue through to stage 4, control. Describe the main communications you intend to carry out in stage 5 and that review and exit, stage 6, will signal the end of the project.

Agree next steps

At the end of the meeting you both need to be sure what the next steps are and who will be carrying them out. In most cases you, as the project manager, will be preparing the meeting notes and prepare the TOR for the project. You may say:

- Using these meeting notes I will prepare a draft TOR.

PROJECT STAGE 1: DEFINE

- What do you see as our next steps?
- During the meeting we discussed ... Should we agree and action these?
- When should we schedule these next steps?

As your sponsor defines a project:

- Write down and agree the proposed project objectives with your sponsor.
- Ask questions, and listen for 80 per cent of the time.
- Develop your own list of standard questions you will ask at initial project meetings.
- If you do not have the time to commit to the project because of other work, say so now!

Structure of meetings

There are three parts to a meeting, before, during and after. Each one of these parts has to be managed in order to get the most out of it. There are also a number of other things you need to understand or practise to make meetings work for you.

Before a meeting

Before the meeting starts you should consider the following:

- What do you want to get out of the meeting?
- Do you have to be there?
- Who will attend?
- How long the meeting will last?
- Who will be the chairperson?
- What will the agenda items be?

During a meeting

During a meeting you want to ensure the following:

- You get out of it what you want.

- You know who all the players are.
- The right people are given the tasks that come out of a meeting.
- Everyone knows who is doing what.
- Someone is taking notes.
- You or someone manages the time.
- Difficult questions get asked rather than avoided.

After a meeting

After the meeting is over consider the following:

- Have the meeting notes been written up and circulated?
- Was the meeting useful or a waste of time?
- Make sure you complete the tasks you were allocated.

Essential meeting rules

Here are a number of essential meeting rules to consider.

Keep in control

Holding effective meetings keeps you in control. Drive them by:

- Introducing yourself and any of your colleagues.
- If needed, break the ice by offering refreshments.
- Say why you are at this meeting.
- Make sure others agree with why you are holding this meeting.
- Agree how long the meeting should be.
- Have a draft agenda prepared.
- Keep people to the main discussion points.
- Remind people of the time if discussions overrun.
- Take your own notes and record the date, time, place, who was there, the subject and main agreed points.
- Use a template to ensure you ask the right questions.

Start and finish on time

Customers hate to wait. They will not have much confidence in you if you are constantly late for meetings.

Do not hold side meetings

You may be discussing a very important point that others in the meeting need to hear. Holding side meetings signals to others that they can do the same.

Keep to your agenda

The agenda acts as a reminder to all present of the topics to be covered and how much there is left to be covered at any one time. This should be regularly referred to during the meeting and is a good way of controlling the discussion of the agenda items. Consider the following:

- Bring your own. If you are going to someone else's meeting, bring along your agenda items in case they are not already included.
- Ask others for their agandas. If you are running a meeting, be prepared to include other people's agendas with yours.
- Watch the clock. Allocate time to the agenda items and stick to them.
- Hidden agendas. Some people will be positive at meetings and others will be negative. Find out why. Watch out for hidden agendas and ask yourself 'Who is driving this meeting?'

Agree actions

At the end of the meeting agree who will be doing what, and when the next meeting will be held.

Listen

You should be doing 80 per cent of the listening and 20 per cent of the talking. You need to understand what your customer wants.

Take notes

Get used to writing quick simple notes that you will refer to after the meeting
The most important note to record is a simple description of the objectives.

Be enthusiastic

Build confidence between you and your customer by being enthusiastic and showing interest in the project.

Learn to say 'No'

Quite often we automatically accept work given to us from others without really checking whether we have enough time to complete it. Consider the following:

- If you do not have the time, you will let your customer down. Be polite but firm and do not accept the work.
- If you cannot say 'No', then give your customer a realistic date when you can deliver this additional work.
- If your customer does not accept your delivery date, let them know you will be asking for additional people or equipment to complete the job on time.

Handling meetings

- Prepare a typed agenda before the meeting and circulate to attendees.
- Start and finish your meeting on time.
- At the end of the meeting agree action points and who will do them.
- Do not hold side meetings.

Recording project objectives in the terms of reference

Ensure adequate initial and ongoing discussion, understanding and agreement with management on the cornerstones of the project: Mission, scope, milestones, assumptions, resources, risks, contingency plans and deliverable. (Andreas Schmidt, Business Information Manager, Novartis)

You have now attended at least one meeting with your project sponsor and you are now in a position to create a document called the 'Terms of Reference'. This document contains all the information that defines the project. It is the most visible way in which you demonstrate to your customer/sponsor that you have understood his or her problem and requirements. The TOR serves as the 'contract' between you and your sponsor and will be referenced and updated several times during the life of the project.

In some cases, even the main objectives may change, and these changes must be documented, usually in a change request form, so that the focus for the project is not lost. It is essential that any changes to the TOR is discussed in detail and agreed by your sponsor before being implemented. *No project manager has the power to change the TOR without the express agreement of the sponsor.*

Only when the TOR has been approved by the sponsor can a project truly begin. This approval should be obtained in writing such as a signature on the TOR, but in many cases a written memo, e-mail note or letter will serve as approval by the sponsor to begin the project.

What the terms of reference contain

As the TOR is a structured document, it contains headings where you record information that describes the project's objectives and what you are proposing to do. You also need to highlight any constraints or assumptions you are making and show the key deliverables and milestones involved in your planned results. You will have to indicate your costs and resourcing requirements. The TOR is usually completed after two to three meetings with your sponsor.

Use the template in Chapter 9 (Figure 9.3) to prepare your TOR. The following describes the headings to use and a description of their content.

Client details

Record the sponsor's name, address and contact information.

Start date

Note the proposed start date for the project. Quite often this is left empty until the sponsor agrees to a start date. Sometimes the date is only entered after a detailed schedule is prepared at the planning stage, and very often the start date is determined by working backwards from the end date.

Project name

Keep the project name short and create a memorable acronym that people will easily remember.

Background

This section contains a brief description of the background to the work that needs to be done. You may consider documenting the following:

● Why are you doing this project?
● Note any past problems or other relevant issues.

Keep this section to a maximum of two paragraphs.

Objectives

State the project goals that must be achieved; try to keep this to one sentence per goal. Keep the number of goals to a minimum, preferably one goal only.

Benefits to business

You must understand almost better than the customer/user what the business benefits of the project are. (Alan Goodson, Project Leader, The Dow Chemical Company)

Quite often a separate business benefit case is prepared before the project has started, so only a reference to this document needs to be made. However, if no investigation into the business benefit has been made, you need to identify both tangible and intangible benefits. These may include:

● projected increase in revenue
● projected reduction in costs

- improvements to the business
- increased quality
- reduced waste, work in progress, stock.

Scope/boundary of work

This is the most time-consuming part of the TOR and describes the boundaries or scope of the work to be covered. Clearly identify:

- what will be done
- what will not be done
- which departments will be involved
- any quality standards.

Constraints

Record any constraints that will potentially affect the execution of the project. This section will act as an early warning system and needs to be regularly reviewed. You can also note high-risk events that need consideration. Typical constraints include:

- time
- people
- money
- equipment
- high-risk events
- health and safety issues.

Assumptions

Use this section to state any assumptions you are making. After your first meeting with your sponsor, there will be a number of facts that you do not have. You need to obtain this information at your next meeting and this assumption section will prompt you to ask for it.

This section is especially useful when you are preparing a TOR with other colleagues or your team, as you can avoid disagreements by noting down assumptions being made. If you are not sure whether someone is right, note down the assumption being made. The sponsor will clarify this point at the next meeting.

When your TOR is signed off, there should be no assumptions in it as you will have discussed these with your sponsor. Agreement to each assumption will have been made and other sections in the TOR will have been adjusted.

Reporting

State the sponsor's progress reporting requirements showing:

- who will receive your progress reports.
- when the reports will be delivered.
- how these reports will be presented, as meetings, e-mail, by telephone or on paper.

Deliverables

State the project deliverables indicating:

- what the deliverables will be.
- when they will be delivered.

Dates for deliverables can be noted down as milestones, that is, an event in time that has no duration.

Activity time chart

You should aim to produce a simple activity time chart that shows a list of the main tasks involved in your project, their sequence and the month these tasks will be carried out. You also need to show how long they will take and who will be completing these tasks. Typical tasks will include:

- planning.
- analysis.
- work on deliverables.
- report productions.
- progress meetings.
- review.

Finance

You need to give an initial indication what the project will cost. In your estimate, include the following:

- the fee rate for each resource (e.g. cost/day)
- the total costs for each resource
- the costs for specialist equipment
- the expenses for travel and accommodation
- the sum of the costs and expenses to show the total estimated budget.

Terms of reference

Throughout this book a case study will be used to show the various documents and techniques that are used on a project. The case study involves a fictitious organization called Geld International that wants to start selling its products on the Internet, an area called electronic commerce (e-commerce). Their products include insurance and pensions and they currently sell directly to customers in Europe.

You are a seasoned project manager and work for an independent management consultancy that specializes in project management.

The Marketing Director of Geld International, Oliver Smith-Jones, recently read an article about electronic commerce and believes that this is the way forward for exposing the company's products to a global marketplace, increasing sales without dramatically increased overheads. It also appears to be a natural progression from direct telephone sales.

This case study starts at the point when Oliver Smith-Jones sends a letter to the Sales Director of your organization asking for an investigation into the feasibility for implementing electronic commerce within their organization. This memo is shown in Figure 3.2.

Your Sales Director forwards the memo from Oliver Smith-Jones to you and asks you to manage this project. You request an initial meeting with Oliver Smith-Jones, the project sponsor, to clarify various points and begin to build a positive business relationship. This meeting will be the foundation for preparing the TOR. After attending the meeting, you review the information recorded on the project definition – sponsor meeting form (Figure 9.2) and begin to prepare a TOR. An example of this is shown in Figure 3.3.

GELD INTERNATIONAL

| London | Madrid | Frankfurt | Paris |

DATE: 11 June

TO: Sales Director of your organization

FROM: Oliver Smith-Jones, Marketing Director

RE: Electronic Commerce

CC: ETB, J Worthington

I was very pleased to meet you last week to discuss the above. As you are aware, global presence in the marketplace is vital to the on going success of Geld International. Our physical presence in Europe continues to strengthen with offices in London, Madrid, Frankfurt and Paris.

Our aim is to expand our organization world-wide by trading electronically though the Internet. I understand this is referred to as e-commerce, and we are creating a department specifically to run this part of our organization.

We would welcome your excellent guidance in managing this project and look forward to meeting you and your project manager at our next meeting this week.

Best regards

Oliver Smith-Jones

Figure 3.2   Memo from the Marketing Director commissioning the project

PROJECT STAGE 1: DEFINE

Electronic Commerce: TERMS OF REFERENCE
Geld International

Sponsor Name	Date
Oliver Smith-Jones	20 June

Project Manager Name	Sponsor Address
Emily Goodson	Geld International Centre House 1 Major Place, London S12

Project Title	Start Date
E-commerce Pilot (ECP)	1 July

Background

Geld International is a banking organization that has an established base in Europe. The executive of Geld International see the need to globalize the organization by offering a limited range of products for sale through the Internet.

Objectives

To identify and investigate all the elements needed to sell Geld International products on the Internet.

Benefits to Business

Increase market share.
Create presence in the global marketplace.
To achieve a return on investment within two years.
To generate a new revenue stream using existing products.

Scope/Boundary of Work

1. Create a research team consisting of a mixture of Geld International personnel and people from your organization.
2. Interview executive in London, Madrid, Paris and Frankfurt.
3. Only consider selling insurance products.
4. Recommend a structure for a new department that will be created specifically to manage this new direct selling method.
5. Carry out desk research to gather information on best practices from other people's experience.
6. Investigate legal aspects of direct selling across international boundaries.
7. Attend international conference on e-commerce.
8. Interview internet experts in IT departments in Geld International across Europe.
9. Recommend technical infrastructure.

Figure 3.3 Terms of Reference for the electronic commerce project

Constraints to be confirmed

1. Available budget has not been identified. This project will determine the setup and running costs for establishing e-commerce for Geld International.
2. No delivery date for setting up e-commerce has been agreed. A project schedule will be created that will show the timescales.

Assumptions to be confirmed

1. Direct reporting will be made to Oliver Smith-Jones. In his absence, reporting is to be made to his executive personal assistant, Pat.
2. The steering committee will be created by the sponsor after the approval of this TOR. This will have representation from the technical, customer and business personnel.
3. Issues from the project team will be escalated to the sponsor for resolution.
4. Changes to the TOR will be documented and must be approved or rejected by the sponsor.

Project Reporting Method

1. Weekly progress report will be sent to the sponsor, Oliver Smith-Jones.
2. A meeting will be held every three weeks with the steering committee.

Deliverables and Milestones

1. New department report.
2. Legal report.
3. E-commerce research report.
4. Technical Infrastructure report.

Figure 3.3 (*continued*)

48

Activity Time Chart For Project:

Activity	Who	Effort	Total	Month	1	2	3	4	5	6	7	8
Planning	A,B,C	2d	6d		**							
Build Team	A,B,C	5d	15d			***						
Work on deliverables												
– New dept report	B,C	20d	40d						*******			
– Legal report	B,C	20d	40d						*******			
– Ecom research rpt	B,C	20d	40d						*******			
– Tech Infrastucture	B,C	20d	40d						*******			
Final Presentations	B,C	10d	20d									**
Progress Meetings	A	5d	5d		*	*	*	*	*			

Total Effort:	206 days

Estimated Costs

Resource Name: Project Manager(A) Rate: 1000 Effort: 12d Cost: 12,000
Resource Name: Internal Team(B) Rate: 1000 Effort: 97d Cost: 97,000
Resource Name: Client Team(C) Rate: 0 Effort: 97d Cost:
Resource Name: Rate: Effort: Cost:

Equipment Name: Cost:

Expenses: Cost: 10,000
Expenses: Cost:

Total Estimated Costs: 119,000

Approval

Sponsor Name:_____ Department: _____

Signature:_____ Date: _____

Figure 3.3 (*continued*)

4 Project stage 2: plan

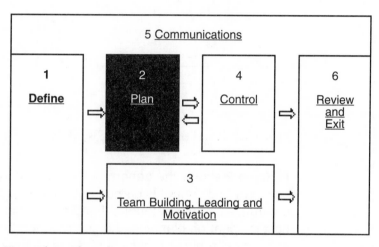

Figure 4.1 Plan

Now that the terms of reference have been agreed with the sponsor, a detailed plan of the work has to be prepared.

A project manager often considers how much of his or her time needs to be spent on preparing a plan. Too much time planning for a simple project may be considered a waste, but too little time on a complex project would introduce unnecessary risk. A simple project could be viewed as one with a small budget, or a small number of people involved. A complex project would be the opposite, where the budget would be large, more than three or four people involved in the team and, perhaps, where there are a number of different locations involved in the project.

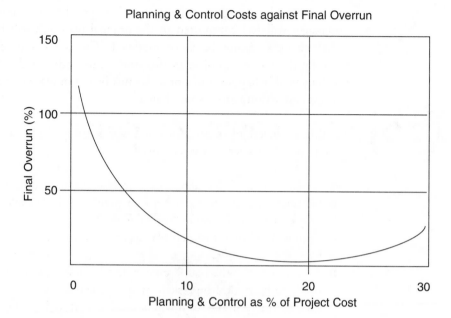

Figure 4.2 One benefit of planning is reducing the final overrun cost

Figure 4.2 shows the general relationship between how much planning and control is carried out on a project and the final cost overrun. As a rule of thumb, if less than 5 per cent of the project cost is spent on planning and control, then the project manager can expect a high probability of doubling the original budget. About 15 to 20 per cent of the project cost should be allocated to planning and control. If too much time is spent on planning and control, for example, over 25 per cent, then there is a danger that the final project budget will exceed original estimates.

Quite often, a newly appointed project manager will have a number of objections towards spending any significant time on planning a project. The most common complaint is that planning requires a lot of work and this takes time – time that can be spent on completing tasks required by the project.

Another complaint is that planning is not viewed as being productive by many people involved in a project. It is not action; it is not producing anything! Planning is a pretty chart that gets pinned on a wall at the beginning of a project and never gets updated again. It will change within a few days of starting a project, so why create a plan in the first place.

A final complaint that is often heard is that the original plan is fixed and cannot be changed, as the sponsor has agreed to it. The project manager will feel committed to the original plan and will believe that changes cannot be accommodated. The concept of change during the life of a project in this case is not understood. Change will inevitably happen and a process must be put in place to capture, assess and action requests for change.

All these objections to preparing and working with a plan are overcome when a project manager considers the following:

- A plan is a 'map' that allows us to reach the project objectives.
- Getting the team to participate in preparing a plan allows the project manager to secure 'buy-in' to the project by the team. The team will feel that it is their plan as they contributed to preparing it.
- As a minimum, the plan contains detailed information on what needs to be done (the tasks), by whom and by when. Without this information, the team will not know what to do and when to do it by.
- No corrective action can be take during a project unless there is something to refer to. This reference point, or baseline, is the plan.

Above all, a plan is a tool or business device that allows the objectives of a project, as defined in the TOR, to be achieved. It is a 'living' document that can be changed during the life of the project.

Earlier in this book we have said that a plan contains the following seven elements:

1 Creating a work breakdown structure (WBS).
2 Creating the team structure and individual responsibilities.
3 Estimating effort and duration for each task.
4 Preparing the schedule.
5 Allocating resource to tasks.
6 Determining the budget.
7 Risk analysis and contingency.

Each of these elements will now be discussed in detail, using the case study to show us how to prepare the necessary documentation to complete our plan.

Creating a work breakdown structure

Break down each insurmountable giant mound of work into reasonably bite-sized chunks so that the people in your project team can gobble them up easily. What's a reasonable chunk? Something of a size manageable by the person or people about to do the work. (Dalim Basu, Project Manager, ITN)

Preparing a WBS is a technique that allows the project manager to break down the total work of the project, described in the TOR into themes, or main groups of work. These themes, or groups, are then subdivided into tasks and then sub-tasks. The final sub-task should be viewed as a piece of work, or work package, that an individual or team can deliver to a budget, where they define and control the day-to day activities to an agreed quality standard.

Preparing a final report and presentation that uses several other reference documents, requires a significant amount of organizing by a team member to complete and deliver this report and presentation. Exactly when and how this work is carried out is the responsibility of the team member, and all the sub-tasks needed to complete this work do not need to be identified in a WBS. It is sufficient to identify 'Final report and presentation' in the WBS, a task that can then be assigned to the team member.

In another example of how much detail a WBS should describe, consider the construction of an office building. It would be acceptable to identify a task labelled 'Install lift' and not to break this task down any further. This task can be assigned to the building contractor who would then identify and manage the design and construction of the lift to an agreed budget, time and quality specification. This is an example of a team, rather than an individual, carrying out the lowest task described in a WBS.

The approach in constructing a WBS is similar to building an organization chart. There are many popular software applications that allow us quickly to construct organization charts, and these can easily be used to prepare a WBS.

After preparing a TOR, it is very tempting to use one of many excellent project management software packages to create and record a WBS. If at all possible, avoid using a computer at this stage and use the technique described in this section to create a WBS. There are two main reason why this is suggested:

1 Creating a WBS is a great exercise to begin building and motivating the team. Everyone feels they are contributing to the creation of the plan. All that is needed is a meeting room, a flipchart, pens and adhesive notepaper. Ask each team member to note down any tasks they think are needed that meet the project objectives. This is a challenge that the team will like, and the project manager will harness the experience of the team at this early stage.
2 The WBS is an excellent communication device that can be used after it is complete. At a glance, anyone looking at the WBS will see the entire work needed to complete the project. They will also see significant detail of each main phase of the work as they inspect the hierarchical structure of the WBS from top to bottom.

Here are the basic rules for creating a WBS:

- The first box at the top of the WBS tree should show the project name, or an acronym of the project name (as in Figure 4.3).
- The descriptions of the work in each box should be brief and easily understood.
- Do not subdivide all the work to the same lowest level.
- WBS does not show any interdependencies.
- WBS does not show any timescales.

Figure 4.3 is an example of a WBS using our e-commerce case study from Chapter 3. When this was created, not enough information was known about creating a new department within the organization, so it was decided to keep the WBS simple by just identifying the phase as 'New Department'. This is acceptable, because this phase of the work will be allocated to the HR department where a sub-project will be created. A TOR will be generated by HR followed by a plan to create the new department.

Another thought about creating a WBS. It is natural to consider the items that need to be delivered and to record these in the WBS. There are several other ways to create a WBS. These include:

PROJECT STAGE 2: PLAN

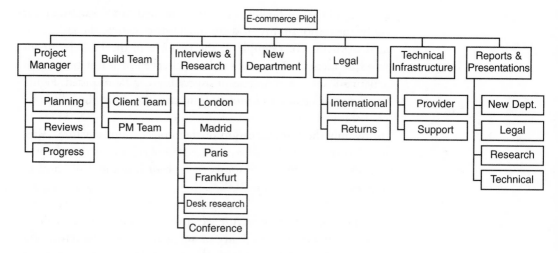

Figure 4.3 Work breakdown structure for the E-commerce Pilot Project

- by geographic structure
- product component structure
- functional structure.

The geographic structure of an organization, such as 'Northern' and 'Southern' regions, may be visualized when creating a WBS and the deliverables from each sub-geographical structure considered. If a project involves creating a product made up of several components, then the WBS may be created showing all the main components and sub-components that different teams would need to work on. Finally, a WBS may be created showing the work that needs to be carried out by the different functions in the organization, such as Finance, Production, IT, Marketing, HR and so on.

Creating the team structure and individual responsibilities

Split project teams into sub-teams of not more than eight people. (Peter Suhr-Jessen, Project Manager, Novo Nordisk)

After the WBS has been completed, an initial team structure can be created and presented as an organization chart. Not all the resource names can be identified at this stage, but their function can, and it will be the responsibility of these functions to deliver the tasks allocated to them. For example, if the resource in the IT department cannot be identified as named individuals, then their functions, such as 'network specialist' or 'telecom specialist' can be recorded. Figure 4.4 shows the creation of project team structure from the WBS.

This is only the initial creation of the project team structure. After the effort of each task is identified, as described later in this chapter, the number of individual resources can be identified and allocated to each task.

After the project team structure has been created, a chart describing the authority and responsibility of key members can be drawn up. These key members are not limited to the project team itself, but can include others such as the sponsor, stakeholders, users or customers, suppliers, company departments, consultants or other contractors.

It is the process of creating this chart that will generate a great deal of discussion and begin bonding the team together. Quite often the sponsor is invited to participate in this discussion, as he or she is the person that must agree to the overall authority and responsibility of each person or group identified on the chart.

To create an authority chart, first agree the type of authorities that will be created.

Here is a list of four types of authorities that may be considered:

● must approve
● must be informed
● must be consulted
● must prepare.

Different types of projects, or processes within a project, will attract different types of authorities and responsibilities. In a project that creates a product, there may be authorities such as 'must assemble' or 'must check'. In other projects that deal with security issues there may be 'must record information' or 'must hold key'.

The next step in creating an authority chart is to agree on the tasks that will be considered, usually from the WBS, and to agree on the

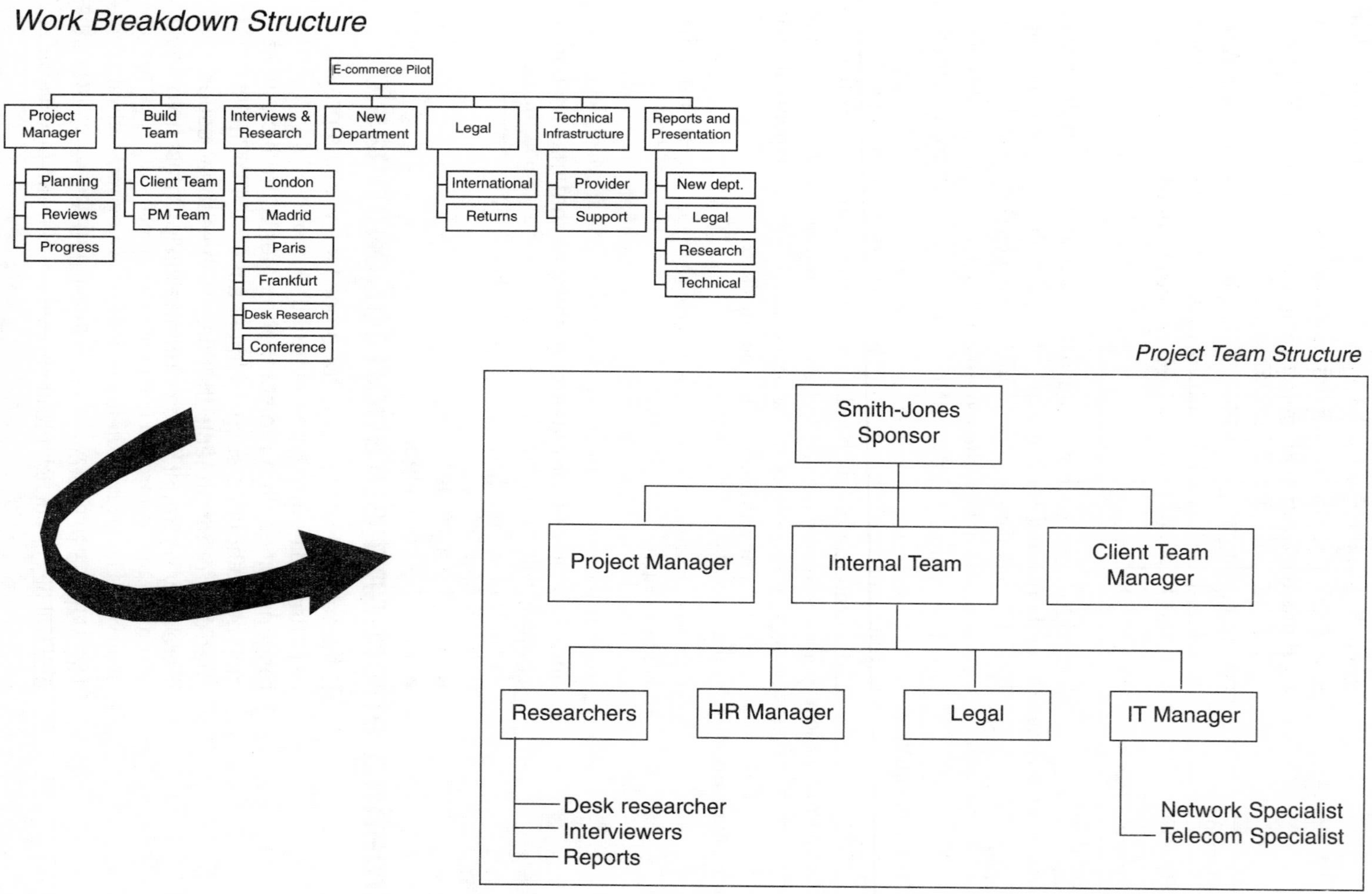

Work Breakdown Structure

Figure 4.4 Creating a project team structure from a work breakdown structure

	Sponsor	Project Manager	Researchers	HR Manager	Legal	IT Manager	Presenter
Planning	□	✗	○	○	○	○	○
Reviews	△	✗	△	△	△	△	△
Progress Meetings	△	✗	△	△	△	△	△
Build Team		✗					
Interviews & Research	□	△	✗				
New Department	△	△		✗			
Legal	△	△			✗		
Tech Infrastructure	△	△				✗	
Report	□	△					✗
Client Presentations	□	△	△	○	○	○	✗

□ Must approve
△ Must be informed
○ Must be consulted
✗ Must prepare

Figure 4.5   Authority chart for the E-commerce Pilot Project

resource that will have different levels of authority. The team carrying out the exercise to create the authority chart then debates the authorities and responsibilities required for each task and which resource will be given these authorities and responsibilities. An example of such a chart can be seen in Figure 4.5.

Estimating effort and duration for each task

Now is the time to introduce the power and flexibility of a computer. Great care must be exercised in selecting the appropriate software package that will be used to complete the plan and then to control the project. The classic mistake when selecting a software package is to think that it will provide a rapid step-by-step recipe to planning and control. This rapidness in planning is often not achieved. The great flexibility offered by a variety of software packages is their potential weakness. A project manager inexperienced in using a particular package can easily and quickly change some figures, and then spend the next two to three hours working out why the package does not present information the way the project manager expects.

The golden rule in working with computer packages is to gain experience by initially using paper, then quickly move on to a spreadsheet and, finally, use a software package specifically designed to plan and control projects.

In this book we will begin this process by using paper to record information which can easily be transferred to a spreadsheet. All the information described in this and the next four sections, that are needed to complete a project plan (effort, duration, schedule, budget and risk), can be recorded on two sheets of paper, examples of which are shown in Figures 4.6 and 4.7.

First start by transferring the tasks identified in the WBS to the analysis matrix as shown in Figure 4.6. A blank form is also shown in Chapter 9, Figure 9.4, for you to use throughout the project management process. Once the tasks have been recorded, you need to estimate how long it will take each resource, or team of resources, to complete each task. This is the effort required to complete the task.

After completing your estimates of effort for each task, translate this into the duration each task will take and record this on your analysis matrix.

What is the difference between effort and duration? When estimating effort, think of the time that the task will take to complete assuming no interruptions, breaks, lost or wasted time (no weekends, holidays, sickness, training days etc.) when working on the task. Duration is the time the task actually takes to complete and includes all the lost, wasted or waiting time. Effort drives costs and duration drives the completion date of the project.

As a project manager, whenever you need to estimate the effort and duration for work, always invite the experts in to obtain these figures. They are the people with the experience to give you reasonably accurate figures. Do not be tempted to estimate these figures yourself. The responsibility of the project manager is to provide the tools, techniques and framework to plan and control.

heet No: 1 of 1	Project Title:	E-commerce Pilot Project (ECP)												

Resource name & rate/day: A= Proj Mg £1,000   B= Internal Team £1,000   C= Client Team (no rate)   D=

Description	Depend	Effort A	Effort B	Effort C	Effort D	Duration	Cost A	Cost B	Cost C	Cost D	Total Cost	Probability of Failure H/L/M	Impact on Project H/M/L	Contingency Action (If M/M or above)
1 Project Manager														
1.1 Planning		4	1	1		14	4000	1000			5000	L	H	
1.2 Reviews	1.1	5				56	5000	0			5000	M	H	Hire project assistant
1.3 Progress Meetings	1.1	5				56	5000	0			5000	M	H	Hire project assistant
2 Build Team								0	0		0			
2.1 Internal Team	1.1	5	5	5		14	5000	5000			10000	L	H	
2.2 Client Team	1.1	5		5		14	5000	0			5000	M	H	Hire team building or leadership specialist
3 Interviews & Research								0	0		0			
3.1 London, Madrid, Paris, Frankfurt	2.1		10	5		21	0	10000			10000	M	M	Get senior commitment for interviews
3.2 Desk Research	2.1		5			14	0	5000			5000	L	M	
4 New Department	2.1		5	5		21	0	5000			5000	L	M	
5 Legal								0	0		0			
5.1 International	2.2		10	10		28	0	10000			10000	L	M	
5.2 Returns	2.1		10	10		28	0	10000			10000	L	M	
6 Technical								0	0		0			
6.1 Provider	2.1		5	5		14	0	5000			5000	L	M	
6.2 Support	2.1		15	15		28	0	15000			15000	L	M	
7 Reports & Presentations								0	0		0			
7.1 New Department	4		5	5		14	0	5000			5000	L	H	
7.2 Legal	5.1,5.2		5	5		14	0	5000			5000	L	H	
7.3 Research	3.1,3.2		5	5		14	0	5000			5000	L	H	
7.4 Technical	6.1,6.2		5	5		14	0	5000			5000	L	H	
Total Resource Cost											110,000			
Equipment Cost														
Expenses											10,000			
Estimated Total Project Cost											120,000			

Figure 4.6 Analysis matrix recording tasks, dependencies, effort, duration, costs, risk and contingency

Achieving the correct estimates for effort and duration is the part of planning that can easily be confusing and where several errors can occur.

In a meeting with the experts, asking the question 'How long will it take to create your report?' may be met with a response like 'Three weeks'. If a project manager accepts this value with no further questioning, there is a big chance that a misunderstanding has occurred. A follow-up statement like 'Is that three weeks of solid work?' may get

Sheet No: 1 of 1		Project Title: E-commmerce Pilot Project (ECP)																									

			July				August					Sept					October					November			
ID	Description	Weeks->	1	2	3	4	5	6	7	8	9	10	11	12	13	14	15	16	17	18	19	20	21	22	23	24
1	Project Manager																										
1.1	Planning		∿	∿	A,B,C																						
1.2	Reviews				∿	∿	∿	∿	∿	∿	∿	∿	A														
1.3	Progress Meetings				∿	∿	∿	∿	∿	∿	∿	∿	A														
2	Build Team																										
2.1	Internal Team				∿	∿	A,B,C																				
2.2	Client Team				∿	∿	A,C																				
3	Interviews & Research																										
3.1	London, Madrid, Paris, Frankfurt							∿	∿	∿	B,C																
3.2	Desk Research							∿	∿	B,C																	
4	New Department							∿	∿	∿	B,C																
5	Legal																										
5.1	International							∿	∿	∿	∿	B,C															
5.2	Returns							∿	∿	∿	∿	B,C															
6	Technical																										
6.1	Provider							∿	∿	B,C																	
6.2	Support							∿	∿	∿	∿	B,C															
7	Reports & Presentations																										
7.1	New Department								∿	∿	B,C																
7.2	Legal									∿	∿	B,C															
7.3	Research								∿	∿	B,C																
7.4	Technical									∿	∿	B,C															
														Project complete: 1 Sept												

Resource Plan	Name	Work Level																								
	A- Proj Mgr	1	1	4	4	2	2	2	2	2	2															
	B - Internal Team	1	1	1	1	7	7	5	5	4	2															

Figure 4.7 Time activity chart recording task schedule, project duration and resource plan

a response of 'Yes'. This would indicate that the estimate was for effort and not duration. The next question would be 'Do you have the people to do this work in three weeks?' This latter question will prompt a response that will provide an estimate for the duration of the task, which already has an estimate of three weeks' effort.

Quite often a sponsor will ask the project manager to reduce the time it will take to complete a particular task (i.e. the duration), and may even offer to provide more resource (i.e. effort) to support this request. An inexperienced project manager may instinctively think that 'throwing' more resources at a task will reduce the time that it takes to complete this task. In other words, increasing the effort can reduce the duration of a task. In many cases this is not true. Consider the following:

- Holding a meeting – as you ask more people to attend a meeting (increasing the effort), the meeting time usually increases (increasing effort not decreasing effort) as everyone wants their thoughts to be heard and to contribute positively to the meeting.
- Clearing an old factory site – if one machine can clear the site in ten days, then two machines may clear the site in about five days. Here is a near linear relationship where increasing the effort decreases the duration. However, there will come a point where a maximum number of machines can be used to clear the site, and then there will be insufficient room for them to manoeuvre. Increasing the number of machines beyond this point will not decrease the duration, but will increase the effort and hence the cost for clearing the site. The extra machines will be parked and will not contribute to clearing the site.
- Taking an aeroplane trip – this is fixed duration trip. Increasing the effort by putting more pilots, crew or passengers on the plane will not decrease the duration of the trip!

Estimating effort and duration is not a one-off process. This is only the first time that these estimates have been made, and the project manager will revisit these estimates when allocating resources (putting names to tasks) later in preparing this plan, and then regularly review these estimates during the life of the project.

Preparing the schedule

The project schedule will show when tasks can be carried out and when the project will be completed. Figure 4.7 shows an example of recording information to produce a project schedule on a time activity chart. The same list of tasks appears in the first column as in the analysis matrix shown in Figure 4.6. At the top of the form is the timescale showing the days, weeks or months, and against each task, the duration recorded in the analysis matrix is entered. This gives the first indication of when the project completion date will be. Some further checking is necessary before this can be confirmed, and this is described in the following sections on allocating resource when the resource plan is prepared.

Before the time activity chart can be filled in with the list of tasks and their duration, the dependency of each task on any other task

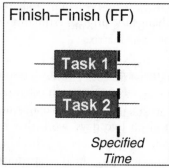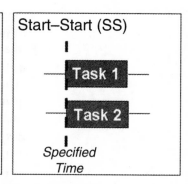

Figure 4.8   Three common types of task dependencies to consider

needs to be identified and recorded. To do this, fill in the 'Depend' column in the analysis matrix. All tasks except the first task in the project must have a dependency. This information is vital in determining the project completion date, and software packages must have this information entered to do this. The most common type of dependency is when one task finishes and the next task starts. This is called a finish–start (FS) dependency. There are also finish–finish (FF) dependencies where both tasks must finish at the same time, and start–start dependencies, where both tasks must start at the same time. These three dependencies are shown in Figure 4.8.

Allocating resource to tasks

 When there are limited resources, both in terms of finance and people, prioritization becomes all-important, as is the need for regular progress reporting. (Howard Gerlis MBCS, Member of Council, British Computer Society)

At this stage of the planning process, the actual individuals who will carry out the tasks may not have been identified. The analysis matrix may only have their function recorded, such as 'Internal Team' or 'Client Team'. As soon as resource names are identified, the plan, in terms of the analysis matrix and activity time chart, has to be updated to include actual names. The main work now is to reconfirm the estimates of effort and duration in the analysis matrix. The resources that have been provided to join the team are not necessarily the ones that were considered or expected when the estimation process took place. Their experience many not be as extensive as was hoped, or their availability may only be part time. This will probably change the original estimation of effort and duration recorded in the analysis matrix.

The final aspect of allocating resource during the preparation of the plan is to ensure that each resource, or team, has not been overallocated work. The project manager needs to make sure that nobody has been given two days' work that has to be completed in a one-day period. This process of checking work allocation is known as resource levelling. At the bottom of Figure 4.7 is the resource plan which checks on resource allocation and allows the project manager to reschedule tasks on the time activity chart to avoid overallocation of work. Rescheduling the work will usually change the project completion date.

The resource plan in Figure 4.7 also identifies the minimum number of resources that are needed to complete each task during a particular week if the project completion date, the end date, cannot be moved. In this example we can see that the project manager will need assistance during weeks 3 and 4, and will probably require assistance during the rest of the project as their allocation is two weeks of work (effort) during every week. The maximum number of resources needed in the internal team will be seven people during weeks 5 and 6. If these people cannot be located, then tasks need to be rescheduled to reduce the numbers in the resource plan.

Determining the budget

The budget required to complete the project is estimated and recorded on the analysis matrix (Figure 4.6). Three figures need to be calculated:

- total resource costs
- equipment costs
- expenses.

At this stage of the planning process each of these costs is an estimate, and the estimates will change as the work on the project begins. The process of estimating these costs is to provide a structured framework for estimating the total project costs. These are presented to the sponsor so that he or she may raise the necessary budget, or make appropriate changes to the scope and deliverables, to reduce the project costs.

Referring to Figure 4.6, the rate for each team is recorded at the top of the analysis matrix. As the client team will be a cost that they already meet, this has been excluded from the project estimates. Next, the effort for each resource, in this case the project manager and the internal team, is calculated and recorded in the appropriate cost column. The total resource costs can now be estimated. A one-line cost for equipment and expenses is provided, although any detailed calculations and estimates can be provided in a separate supporting report. The total estimated project cost can now be recorded and reported to the sponsor.

Risk analysis and contingency

No project will run exactly to plan. Take a risk-based approach to project management and anticipate changes and risks to the project as far ahead as possible. This is a major key to success and will help you when things go wrong. (Paul L'Estrange, Manager – Development Support, Philip Morris)

While preparing your WBS, analysis matrix and activity time chart, you will include tasks or adjust your estimates to make provision for when things go wrong. This contingency planning is an important part of preparing your project plan. However, as a project manager, you will find yourself in a position where you need to defend any contingency arrangements in your project. You may find yourself in front of your sponsor or steering committee presenting your plan and that body-piercing question is put to you:

● 'How much contingency have you included in this project?'

or

● 'Where is your contingency?'

Your response may be:

● 'We've added 10 per cent extra time to the end of each task.'

or

● 'We've added a task at the end of each phase called 'Contingency' in case we need more time.'

One of the first things your sponsor or steering committee member will do when he or she reviews your plans is to discover where you have added 'extra time', and then they will remove it! The psychology of this is simple, you know your sponsor will try anything to reduce the costs or timescales for delivering the project. So, you expect them to cut 5 to 10 per cent away from your budgeted cost or time. You, in turn, need to add 10 or 20 per cent to your planned budget before you meet because you expect it to be taken away!

This scenario is one of the key areas where projects begin to fail. If you have estimated correctly, you need that time to complete the tasks. You do not want your sponsor or steering committee member to take it way. How do you overcome this dangerous situation?

You need to justify to your sponsor or steering committee member exactly where and why you have added 'extra time' in your project plan. This is done by carrying out a risk analysis to identify all those tasks that are high risk and then create new tasks that are contingencies in case things go wrong. By this process you are specifically identifying two types of tasks:

● work that *must* be done to reduce the risk of the project failing
● work that *might* be needed if things go wrong.

Work that has been identified as 'must be done' will increase the project budget, but they will reduce the risk of project failure. In other cases, a series of tasks could be identified as 'work that might done', which are solutions to problems when things go wrong. No additional cost is required at the this stage in the project, but might be required if things go wrong; 'Forewarned is forearmed' is a very appropriate saying.

How to measure risk

Risk and contingency need to be carried out during the planning stage of a project, although this step is often omitted because it is often thought to be too difficult or time-consuming to prepare. This is a misconception as the process for preparing a risk analysis only involves the following two steps:

● identifying high-risk tasks
● preparing contingency tasks.

Identifying high-risk tasks

To carry out a risk analysis for each task on your plan, you will need to:

● determine the *probability of failure* of that task using a high, medium or low scale
● determine the *impact on the project* if the task fails using a high, medium or low scale.

After you have recorded your risk assessment for each individual task, you need to highlight those tasks that have a combination of medium (M) or high (H) ranking for both the 'probability of failure' and 'impact on the project'. These are your high-risk tasks and a contingency plan of action needs to be made for each one. Record the contingency actions as tasks in your analysis matrix.

In our case study, the analysis matrix in Figure 4.6 shows a typical risk and contingency assessment, which are recorded in the last three columns. For each task, the probability of failure was recorded as H, M or L, and then the impact on the project was also recorded as H, M or L should the task fail. The risk assessment highlighted four tasks having a combination of MM, MH, HM, or HH and these were:

● Project Manage – Reviews
● Project Manage – Progress Meetings
● Build Team – Client Team
● Interviews and Research – London, Madrid, Paris, Frankfurt

Preparing contingency tasks

After completing the risk assessment, a contingency plan can be created to reduce the risk of these four tasks failing.

In our case study in Figure 4.6, for the first two tasks a suitable contingency would be to hire a project assistant who would be responsible for all the logistics to ensuring the project reviews and progress meetings are held. Tasks like sending reminders to participants, preparing an agenda, recording meeting minutes and circulating actions arising from the meetings would need to be actioned.

To reduce the risk of the client team not performing well, a consultant specializing in team-building and leadership may be hired.

For the final high-risk task, completing a number of interviews across Europe, commitment from senior members of the organization would have to be gained before these interviews took place. A communications exercise may be the answer raising the profile of the project to the senior management team.

- Do not carry out a risk analysis by yourself. Get the team to participate as you need to generate as many different alternative contingency tasks as possible.
- If possible, let your sponsor know that you have carried out a risk analysis before they ask you to reduce your timescales by 10 per cent.

The complete plan

All the elements of the plan are now complete and this needs to be presented to the sponsor for approval before communicating the plan to the team.

The plan consists of a work breakdown structure, authority chart, analysis matrix and time activity chart. From these reports we know what needs to be done, when and by whom. We also have a team structure, their authority and an estimate of how much the project will cost. High-risk tasks have been identified and contingency plans drawn up.

The plan is a collection of living documents and will change over the life of the project. Managing this change process will be discussed in Chapter 8 when we consider how to control a project. We now need to build, lead and motivate our team which is discussed in the next three chapters.

- Next time you are asked to start a project, use a terms of reference template to ask the correct questions.
- If you are asked to change something in your project, record this on a change template and send this to your customer.

5 Project stage 3: team-building

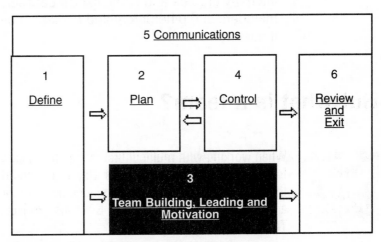

Figure 5.1 Team-building, leading and motivating

The other main component in managing projects involves the process of building, leading and motivating teams. When it comes to people and relationships we enter a very different arena to that which involves defining our Terms of Reference and conducting risk and probability assessments. Applying project management tools and techniques is one thing, managing people is another. As we all know, managing people in the working environment involves a complex world where drives and emotions such as ambition, motivation, competition, power, control, co-operation, trust and mistrust come into play.

No project can be managed without the need to manage relationships. These will normally involve your project sponsor, his or her staff, the stakeholders and your project team. They therefore present a very challenging aspect of the project manager's role. Fail to manage people and we fail to manage projects. So for the vast majority of project managers, managing the people elements is often the most demanding aspect of the role.

In any project situation our people management experiences will almost invariably vary from one project to another but the essential factors that we will need to cope with include:

- defining the leadership role and style – deciding on the right amount of task control and relationship support provided to the team to bring out the best of individual talents
- managing the various group dynamics – this includes the interplay of roles and relationships between the various team members and other interested parties. In other words building the team.

But what is a team?

When working with multicultural teams, make allowances for different responses to issues. Dig deeper and discover the real problems before making judgements on progress and plans for future work. (Alan Goodson, Project Leader, The Dow Chemical Company)

A team can be defined as a collection of individuals who have a specific purpose and are committed to the following:

- achieving a goal
- high performance
- caring for each other
- achieving more collectively than through any one individual – this is what is often termed 'synergy'.

Team development: the classic phases

In developing a fully functioning team any project manager will need to understand the four distinct stages that most groups experience and work through on their way to becoming a fully integrated team. These stages were developed from research and are generally recognized to remain true for most groups. How quickly a team moves through the various stages may well depend on the complexity and difficulties involving and surrounding the project as well as the previous experience the project team members have of working with each other. There can be no set time predictions about these phases, only recognition and understanding that they do occur and that they have to be managed. A key element of beginning to understand the people-side of projects requires the project manager to be aware of these stages and to take appropriate action to guide a team through them.

Stage 1: forming

This involves the team coming together, and is characterized by a certain degree of uncertainty. Sometimes the atmosphere at this stage can be rather strained, particularly if people do not know each other. Superficiality and politeness are demonstrated as people begin the process of getting to know each other. But at this forming stage of team building, relationships generally remain impersonal as people display a certain degree of anxiety or nervousness about what might happen to them.

For the project manager the real objective is to get the team through this rather uncertain phase by getting the team together and effecting some strong introductions. The use of 'start up' type activities such as a small party or other fun and social-type event can often help some people by accelerating this introductions phase. At the same time the project manager needs to establish and set out clear goals and objectives for the team, clarifying individual roles, expectations and objectives along with the identification of stakeholders and other interested parties. Communicating the Terms of Reference is an obvious way of establishing focus for the team.

Stage 2: storming

The storming phase of any team's development can often be a worrying time for a project manager. Principally this is because it often feels as though the whole team is losing all sense of cohesion and spirit. Disagreements, conflicts and arguments are a common characteristic of the storming stage. 'Feeling stuck' and 'getting nowhere' are descriptions of what it sometimes feels like to be caught up in this phase.

The difficulty during a storming phase is that people are often trying to secure positions within the team. For some, they may be challenging the project methodology or approach whilst others maybe trying to influence some other aspect of the project. This sort of behaviour, which often results from having enthusiastic and committed people on board, can naturally generate tensions. Strong personalities and different ideas clash. This debate or argument absorbs a great deal of time and vital energy. Consequently a loss of impetus or progress maybe experienced by some team members. As a result they get fed up. Some people may even seek to drop out altogether and others may try to form sub-groups or cliques. Suffice to say that to the inexperienced project manager it may feel as though you have lost control and that the team is breaking up in front of your eyes.

In managing any storming stage the first thing to do is to recognize that it is actually happening. So take time out to think about what you may have been observing. Then analyse the symptoms. What is happening? What are people trying to do?

The second action for dealing with a storming phase requires the project manager to remain calm and to see the process as an inevitable part of the team's development. At this stage you will need to employ listening and conflict management skills to ensure that everyone has their say in a reasoned and controlled manner. A 'free for all' argument is likely to be viewed negatively by everyone and as the manager you want to avoid the storming stage continuing into the future as inevitably this will lead to problems.

At some stage the team needs to move on and to do this the project manager must focus his or her efforts on re-establishing a leadership role and restating the aims and objectives of the project itself. Individual roles and responsibilities will also need to be clarified. In effect it requires the project manager to move the team on from a 'how' to a 'what we need to do' perspective.

It is important to recognize the storming stage as a perfectly natural phase that teams go through. Despite the unnerving nature that some teams might show when storming, it is a perfectly healthy side to any team's development. Indeed it is a common characteristic of many failed business teams that they never allowed themselves the right to storm. Such team behaviour is often characterized by subtle game-playing and hidden agendas, whereby everyone knows there is a problem but no one is prepared to confront the real issue.

Stage 3: norming

As the necessary storming phase reaches its conclusion most successful teams will begin to embark on the process of norming. A clear sense of purpose, order and sharing starts to emerge. Team members constructively begin to ask for and give opinions to each other. A practical atmosphere of give and take begins to unfold. The acceptance of roles and responsibilities becomes clear. Decisions are taken through reasoned discussion and people get down to the business and tasks in hand.

At this stage the role of the project manager is to build on the prevailing atmosphere. Supporting people along with giving and receiving feedback and building a positive working climate become critical activities. As a project manager you may want to discuss how the team is working and generally be prepared to put more management emphasis on asking rather that telling. At this stage teams are also more capable of confronting difficulties. By managing in this way you will find that the various roles and boundaries within the group are more clearly established and maintained. In turn, the unity and solidarity of the team begins to grow. This helps the team prepare for the next phase of development.

Stage 4: performing

The reality for many teams in today's world is that they remain for the most part in the norming phase of their development. That is to say they perform well and deliver in a professional manner but that they never really excel. The performing phase of a team's development is the phase that we all aspire to, as it captures the best of people's abilities in working together. The performing phase is characterized by unity, confidence, maturity and high energy. In effect it is people working at their best, displaying excellence, mutual support, flexibility, spirit and pride. It is a phase that most teams momentarily hit but fail to achieve on an ongoing basis.

For a team to operate at this level the individuals need to display very high levels of interpersonal skills. High-performance teams are comfortable discussing almost anything with each other. That is an attribute that cannot be said of the other phases. The ability to give and take tough feedback and confront difficult issues without the fear of upsetting colleagues or destroying the team's morale is a powerful characteristic of this phase.

As for the project manager's role, it takes on an almost new meaning. In a high-performance team the manager's role is very much subservient to the team. The manager almost becomes a coach or facilitator. After all the people being managed not only know exactly what they have to do but are also highly skilled, motivated and energized to complete the work. In such circumstances the manager's role is to create the conditions to enable the team to perform. This will involve a heavy focus on delegation and co-ordination rather than controlling the project in a directive manner. Remember that interdependence and high levels of trust are key characteristics of the performing phase.

Write down your answers to the following questions:

○ *What are my essential strengths and development needs as a leader?*
○ *Am I clear and precise in my communications regarding all aspects of the project?*
○ *Do I adequately ensure that all team members are kept up to date on the project and all relevant facts and issues?*
○ *Do I effectively control strong team members whilst at the same time cultivating the quieter and more introverted members of the team?*
○ *How well do I clarify any misunderstandings?*
○ *Do I provide regular and timely updates on all matters of progress?*
○ *Can I generate a fun and challenging atmosphere?*

High-performance teams

Research into high-performance teams has revealed a number of common behavioural characteristics:

- There is an informal but highly involved working atmosphere.
- Discussions are focused.
- There is a common commitment to clear objectives.
- Listening is high.
- Criticism of others is delivered in a constructive way.
- Disagreements are voiced and worked through.
- Decisions are reached largely through discussion and consensus.
- People are direct and will share their feelings with each other.
- Actions as well as roles and responsibilities are shared.
- If there is a leader, this leadership role can change within the team if particular expertise is required.
- The team is self-critical – reviewing both successes and failures.

Check your team's performance against the above. Consider what you need to do to move towards the characteristics of high-performance teams.

Team roles and functions

Before assigning tasks to people take out real time to assess individual capabilities – skills, knowledge and attitudes. Ask yourself have you got the right people? (Dennis O'Gorman, Senior Project Manager, Fitzpatrick Contractors)

Another key element of managing project teams involves the allocation of key roles and functions to team members. It is essential at the outset of any project that the roles needed successfully to carry out the project are identified and properly allocated to the various team members. So deciding the 'what' and 'who' of the project team becomes a vital first task in managing the people aspects of a project team.

In Chapter 11, we have identified and discussed the various roles of the project manager's work as encompassing the following competencies:

- administrator
- analyst

- negotiator
- communicator – verbal and written
- motivator
- listener
- decision-maker.

But whilst those are the attributes of the manager any project team will also need the various team members to bring competencies and attributes to the group. Any effective project team will want the following types of people:

- *Ideas person* – someone who generates new and radical approaches to problems. An original and innovate thinker who challenges conventional approaches.
- *Detail person* – someone who has an eye for details, who can spot mistakes and errors and challenge on the fine print.
- *Team-builder and energizer* – a team member capable of motivating others within a project team, capable of getting people involved, enthusiastic and excited. A real asset when a team is experiencing difficulty or conflicts.
- *Worker* – this is the person who is happy to simply get on with things in an efficient, competent and trouble-free manner. Such people have a high concern for productivity and structure. In effect they deliver without fuss. The backbone of any project team.

Are there any roles missing from your group (which, if fulfilled, would improve the group's performance)?

Belbin's team types

Whilst the above types are very general they set us thinking about team roles and the contribution these roles make to any team. One of the best pieces of work that has ever been completed on understanding teams and the various roles that people can play in them has been conducted by Dr Meredith Belbin. For many years he has conducted detailed research on team dynamics. His work, which has attracted global recognition, has enabled him to develop a typology that can assist all team managers. It is an approach to understanding teams that is particularly helpful to project managers. The benefit of

Belbin's work is that it provides not only the project manager but also team members with a clear means of understanding:

- our own individual contribution to the team
- how other team members contribute
- how best to allocate activities and tasks amongst the team
- where gaps in the team composition might exist and how best to manage them.

Once we understand our own team roles and their strengths and weaknesses as defined by Belbin, we have a mechanism by which we can, as project managers, improve the balance of our teams and their overall effectiveness.

Belbin's team roles: questionnaire

Directions for completing the questionnaire

For each section allocate a total of ten points among the sentences that you think best reflect or describe your behaviour. The points you allocate may be distributed among several sentences: in extreme cases they might be distributed among all the sentences or ten points may be given to a single sentence. After having worked through the questionnaire enter your points in the table at the end of the questionnaire. Then add up the scores vertically to obtain your scores for each of Belbin's types.

I What I believe I can contribute to a team:
- (a) I think I can quickly see and take advantage of new opportunities.
- (b) I can work well with a very wide range of people.
- (c) Producing ideas is one of my natural assets.
- (d) My ability rests in being able to draw people out whenever I detect they may have something of value to contribute to group objectives.
- (e) My capacity to follow through has much to do with my personal effectiveness.
- (f) I am ready to face temporary unpopularity if it leads to worthwhile results in the end.
- (g) I am quick to sense what is likely to work in a situation with which I am familiar.
- (h) I can offer a reasoned case for alternative courses of action without introducing bias or prejudice.

II If I have a possible shortcoming in teamwork it could be that:

(a)   I am not at ease unless meetings are well structured, controlled and generally well conducted.

(b)   I am inclined to be too generous towards others who have a valid viewpoint that has not been given a proper hearing.

(c)   I have a tendency to talk a lot once the group gets on to new ideas.

(d)   My objective outlook makes it difficult for me to join in readily and enthusiastically with colleagues.

(e)   I am sometimes seen as forceful and authoritarian if there is need to get something done.

(f)   I find it difficult to lead from the front, perhaps because I am overresponsive to the group atmosphere.

(g)   I am inclined to get too caught up in ideas that occur to me and so lose track of what is happening.

(h)   My colleagues tend to see me as worrying unnecessarily over detail and the possibility that things may go wrong.

III When involved in a project with other people:

(a)   I have an aptitude for influencing people without pressurizing them.

(b)   My general vigilance prevents careless mistakes and omissions being made.

(c)   I am ready to press for action to make sure that meetings do not waste time or lose sight of the main objectives.

(d)   I can be counted on to produce something original.

(e)   I am always ready to back a good suggestion in the common interest.

(f)   I am keen to look for the latest in new ideas and developments.

(g)   I believe others appreciate my capacity for cool judgement.

(h)   I can be relied upon to see that all essential work is organized.

IV My characteristic approach to group work is that:

(a)   I have a quiet interest in getting to know colleagues better.

(b)   I am not reluctant to challenge the views of others or to hold a minority view myself.

(c)   I can usually find a line of argument to refute unsound propositions.

(d)   I think I have a talent for making things work once a plan has to be put into operation.

(e)   I have a tendency to avoid the obvious and come out with the unexpected.

(f)   I bring a touch of perfectionism to any team job I undertake.

(g)   I am ready to make contacts outside the group itself.

(h)   While I am interested in all views, I have no hesitation in making up my mind once a decision has to be made.

V I gain satisfaction in a job because:

(a)   I enjoy analysing situations and weighing up all the possible choices.

(b)   I am interested in finding practical solutions to problems.

(c)   I like to feel I am fostering good working relation ships.

(d)   I can exert a strong influence on decisions.

(e)   I can meet people who may have something new to offer.

(f)   I can get people to agree on a new course of action.

(g)   I feel in my element where I can give a task my full attention.

(h)   I like to find a field that stretches my imagination.

VI If I am suddenly given a difficult task with limited time and unfamiliar people:

(a)   I would feel like retiring to a corner to devise a way out of the impasse before developing a line.

(b)   I would be ready to work with the person who showed the most positive approach, however difficult they might be.

(c)   I would find some way of reducing the size of the task by establishing what different individuals might best contribute.

(d)   My natural sense of urgency would help to ensure that we did not fall behind schedule.

(e)   I believe I would keep cool and maintain my capacity to think straight.

(f)   I would retain a steadiness of purpose in spite of the pressures.

(g)   I would be prepared to take a positive lead if I felt the group was making no progress.

(h)   I would open discussions with a view to stimulating new thoughts and getting something moving.

VII With reference to the problems to which I am subject in working in groups:

(a) I am apt to show my impatience with those who are obstructing progress.

(b) Other may criticize me for being too analytical and insufficiently intuitive.

(c) My desire to ensure that work is done properly can hold up proceedings.

(d) I tend to get bored rather easily and rely on one or two particular members to motivate and stimulate me.

(e) I find it difficult to get started unless the goals are clear.

(f) I am sometimes poor at explaining and clarifying complex points that occur to me.

(g) I am conscious of demanding from others the things I cannot do myself.

(h) I hesitate to get my points across when I run up against real opposition.

Interpretation of scores

Allocate the scores from the above questions into Table 5.1. Then add up the points in each column to give a total team-role distribution score.

Table 5.1 Scores

Section	CW	CH	SH	PL	RI	ME	TW	CF
I	g	d	f	c	a	h	b	e
II	a	b	e	g	c	d	f	h
III	h	a	c	d	f	g	e	b
IV	d	h	b	e	g	c	a	f
V	b	f	d	h	e	a	c	g
VI	f	c	g	a	h	e	b	d
VII	e	g	a	f	d	b	h	c
Totals								

Key:
CW – company worker/implementor
CH – chair/co-ordinator
SH – shaper
PL – plant
RI – resource investigator

ME – monitor evaluator
TW – team worker
CF – completer finisher

Source: Reproduced with permission from Dr Meredith Belbin, *Management Teams* and publishers Butterworth-Heinemann.

Belbin originally identified eight types or preferences for working in teams. More recently Dr Belbin has updated his work and revised some of the names allocated to types. The chairman has become the co-ordinator whilst the company worker has become the implementor. At the same time a new type has been introduced. The specialist is someone who provides a very strong but narrow input; specialists are good at providing specialist information and facts. They may not be so good at relating to other team members or detracting themselves from the narrow functional or specialist role. For the purpose of this work we have used the former profiles adopted by Dr Belbin and simply highlighted the name changes that he has introduced. Readers wishing to review the latest work should refer to Dr Belbin's work. *Team Roles at Work*, also published by Butterworth-Heinemann, provides a detailed account of the specialist role.

Some of the essential characteristics of each type are shown below.

The company worker/implementor

Role

- Translates general ideas and plans into practical working objectives.
- Gets down to action.
- Breaks things into tasks and actions.
- Delivers actions and results.

Methods

- Helps ensure the team's objectives have been properly established and that any tasks have been clearly defined.
- Clarifies any practical details and deals with them.
- Maintains a steady, systematic approach.
- Is calm under pressure and reliable.
- Perseveres in the face of difficult and challenging targets.

- Provides practical support to other team members.

Behaviours to avoid

- Unconstructive criticism of other team members' ideas and suggestions.
- Lack of flexibility. Company workers have a high efficiency concern.
- Being resistant to new ideas or innovations.

As a manager, a company worker or implementor's strengths are his or her ability to define objectives and practical details. This type is also very effective in introducing and maintaining procedures and structures. In organizations company workers or implementors are often promoted because of their inherent organizing abilities and skills.

The co-ordinator/chair

Role

- Controls and organizes the activities of the team, making best use of the resources available.
- Pulls the team together.
- Stands back and hovers (as if a helicopter) above the team.
- Able to get people working together.

Methods

- Encourages team members to achieve the team's objectives by helping them to identify their roles and contributions.
- Encourages people to put the team objectives before their own.
- Provides positive feedback on individual performance.
- Smooths over disagreements and interteam competition with keen people insight and understanding. Uses tact and diplomacy to control and manage.
- Identifies weaknesses in the team's composition and organizes and develops the team to neutralize any weaknesses.
- Co-ordinates resources, leads comfortably.
- Exercises self-discipline and perseverance. Acts as a

focal point for the team's effort, especially when under pressure.

● Delegates effectively.

Behaviours to avoid

● Not properly recognizing the abilities of the team. Not using all of the team resources.
● Competing with other team types.
● Failing to add a creative, innovative or challenging aspect to his or her role.
● Abdicating the leadership role in the face of strong competition (particularly from shapers and possibly plants).

As a manager, a chair or co-ordinator is in a good position to lead the team. He or she is comfortable standing back from the detail and can mobilize people to tackle the issues. His or her effective interpersonal skills also ensure that that people will listen and take their lead from an effective chair.

The shaper

Role

● Makes things happen.
● Gives shape and strong direction to the team's activities.
● Injects energy and drive into a team's proceedings.

Methods

● Directs the team's focus, setting objectives and clear priorities.
● Adopts a wide perspective of the team's goals and helps individuals understand their roles and contributions.
● Exerts a strong directive influence on the team's discussions. Summarizes outcomes in terms of objectives and targets.
● Will often appear impatient and in a rush.
● Focuses on progress and achievements. Intervenes when the team wanders from its objectives.
● Challenges others if they are pursuing another direction.
● Can be argumentative and dismissive of people who do not move as fast as him or herself.

Behaviours to avoid

- An overly directive style that assumes undue authority.
- Being too directive when making summaries, appraisals or interventions.
- Not being tactful. Overly blunt or even rude and insensitive to the needs of others.
- Becoming isolated or remote from the team. Losing identity as a team member.
- Being seen as too egotistic.
- Competing with other team members particularly the plant and the monitor evaluator.

A shaper performs best when operating in a team of peers. If in a formal leadership position he or she may well need to adopt more co-ordinator type behaviours. This could require more involvement in routine activities and more self-discipline. Shapers normally focus on a broad-brush approach to getting things done. They have little time for the detail and want to drive forward. They also need to watch that their insensitivity to the needs of others does not in the long term create problems for them. Tact and diplomacy is not always a high priority for shapers.

The plant

Role

- Acts as a primary source of ideas and innovation for the team.
- Creative – an *agent provocateur*.
- An independent perspective.

Methods

- Concentrates his or her attention on the big issues and major strategies.
- Formulates new and often radical ideas and approaches.
- Looks for possible breakthroughs in approaches and methods.
- Times contributions – presenting proposals at appropriate and inappropriate moments.

Behaviours to avoid

- Attempting to demonstrate his or her capabilities over too wide a field.
- Contributing ideas for reasons of self-interest and indulgence rather than the team's needs, and so alienating the team.
- Taking offence when his or her ideas are evaluated, criticized and rejected. Sulking and refusing to make any further contributions to the team.
- Becoming too inhibited about putting ideas forward, especially in dominant, extrovert, or overcritical groups. Being intimidated or alternatively arguing with shapers.

A plant needs to exercise self-discipline and be prepared to listen to team members' comments on his or her ideas and proposals (particularly their monitor evaluator colleague(s)). If found in a leadership role a plant must not let the stresses of controlling the team stifle his or her creative input.

In non-directive roles a plant should expect to be used as a strong team resource; devoting his or her energies and talents towards establishing their role as a creative thinker and ideas person.

The resource investigator

Role

- Explores the team's outside resources and develops useful contacts for the team.
- Harnesses resources for the team.
- A networker and free agent.

Methods

- Make excellent contacts quickly. Develops effective and useful relationships and allies for the team.
- Uses his or her interest in new ideas and approaches to explore outside possibilities. Introduces new people and resources to the team
- Develops his or her role as the team's main point of

contact with outside groups. Keeps up to date with new and related developments that may be helpful to the team's work.

● Helps maintain good relationships in the team and encourages team members to make best use of their talents, especially when the team is under pressure.

Behaviours to avoid

● Becoming too involved with his or her own ideas at the expense of exploring others.
● Rejecting ideas or information before submitting them to the team.
● Relaxing too much when the pressure is off.
● Getting involved in wasteful or unproductive activities. This often results from the resource investigator's natural sociability.

Resource investigators are skilled communicators with a creative outlook. They are vital to helping bring new resources into a team and their networking capabilities make them invaluable.

The monitor evaluator

Role

● Analyses ideas and suggestions.
● Evaluates ideas and approaches for their feasibility and practical value.
● Deals with facts.
● Introduces a high level of critical thinking ability to any team.

Methods

● Uses high levels of critical thinking ability to assess issues and plans.
● Balances an experimenting outlook with a critical assessment.
● Builds on others' suggestions or ideas. Helps the team to turn ideas into practical applications.
● Makes firm but practical and realistic arguments against the adoption of unsound approaches to problems.

- Is diplomatic when challenging suggestions.

Behaviours to avoid

- Using his or her critical thinking ability at the team's expense.
- Tactless and destructive criticism of colleagues' suggestions. Liable to upset others because of this.
- Negative thinking; allowing critical thinking skills to outweigh his or her openness to new ideas. Provoking a 'You always see reasons why it cannot be done!' type of response.
- Competitive behaviour with others.
- Lowering the team's morale by being excessively critical and objective.
- Ignoring other people's passion or emotional commitment to an idea.

A successful monitor evaluator combines high critical thinking skills with a practical outlook. When a monitor evaluator is a team leader they need to avoid dominating other members of the team and stifling contributions. When in a non-directive role a monitor evaluator has the challenge of making his or her voice heard and not appearing threatening to colleagues. If they can avoid a tendency towards undue scepticism and cynicism monitor evaluators' strengths will help them develop their management capability.

The team worker

Role

- Strong team player and member.
- Helps individual team members to contribute.
- Promotes and maintains team spirit and effectiveness.

Methods

- Applies him or herself to the task.
- Observes the strengths and weaknesses of team members.
- Supports team members in developing their strengths, e.g. builds on suggestions and contributions.

- Helps individuals manage their weaknesses by personal advice and assistance.
- Selfless in outlook.
- Improves team communications and builds relationships.
- Fosters a strong sense of team spirit by setting an example.

Behaviours to avoid

- Competing for status or control in the team.
- Aligning with one team member against another.
- Avoiding conflict situations.
- Delaying tough decisions.

The team worker role can be exercised at different levels within a team. As a manager the team worker should see his or her role as a delegator and developer of people. The team worker's qualities of being conscientious and having perseverance will help ensure that projects are completed on time and to the necessary levels of cost and quality. But team workers have to watch that their sense of duty in wanting to help team members achieve objectives often overrides their concerns for personal status.

The completer finisher

Role:

- Ensures all the team's efforts are as near perfect as possible.
- Ensures that tasks are completed and that nothing is overlooked.
- Injects urgency into problems.
- Attention to detail.

Methods

- Perfectionist – looks for errors or omissions; especially those that may result from unclear responsibilities.
- Works on tasks where attention to detail and precision are important.
- Looks for mistakes in detail.

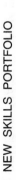

- Actively identifies work or tasks that require more detailed attention.
- Raises the standards of all the team's activities.
- Maintains a sense of urgency and priority.

Behaviours to avoid

- Unnecessary emphasis on detail at the expense of the overall plan and direction.
- Negative thinking or destructive criticism.
- Lowering team morale by excessive worrying.
- Appearing slow moving or lacking in enthusiasm.

A completer finisher role can be exercised at different levels within a team and can easily be combined with another role. As a manager a completer finisher needs to pay careful attention to their delegation skills and to keep unnecessary interference with team members to a minimum. In a junior role a completer finisher will need to develop tact and discretion so as to avoid earning a reputation as a 'nit-picker and worrier.' Completer finishers also tend to possess a nervous drive that needs to be controlled and directed if it is to have positive results.

Table 5.2 provides a summary of the various characteristics of the Belbin types.

Applying the Belbin approach to project teams

Apart from the general understanding of our own individual and colleagues' team preferences we can, as project managers, apply the methodology in several other practical ways. These include using the approach to:

- help in the selection of new project teams
- assist in the selection of new project team members
- facilitate understanding between joint project teams, which combine some strong stakeholder involvement in developing, planning and executing the project. Joint project teams, which do involve stakeholders on a daily basis, are particularly prone to suffer conflict. Using Belbin's questionnaire at the outset of the

Figure 5.2 Belbin team types summary

Type		Typical features	Positive qualities	Allowable weaknesses
Company worker/ Implementor	CW	Solid, dependable, predictable and reliable.	Organizing ability, practical common sense, hard working, self discipline.	Lack of flexibility, unresponsiveness to unproven ideas. Concern to maintain the status quo on efficiency.
Chair/Coordinator	CH	Steady, patient, self confident, controlled, commands respect.	Puts people at ease. Able to get people working together. Good at standing back. A strong sense of objectives and task achievements.	Not necessarily the best at thinking radically or creatively.
Shaper	SH	Energetic, outgoing, tense dynamic, egoistic.	Drive and readiness to make things happen. Challenges ineffectiveness, complacency or self-deception.	Prone to provocation, irritation and impatience. Can be selfish in terms of satisfying self first.
Plant	PL	Individualistic, serious-minded, unorthodox.	Genius, imagination, intellect, knowledge. Concern with the Big Issues.	Up in the clouds, inclined to disregard practical details or protocol. Wrapped up with own ideas.
Resource investigator	RI	Extroverted, enthusiastic, curious, communicative.	A capacity for contacting people and exploring anything new. An ability to respond to challenge and harness resources. Able to sell and excite people.	Liable to lose interest once the initial fascination has passed. Needs to be kept focused.
Monitor evaluator	ME	Unemotional, cautious, data rational and analytical.	Judgement, discretion, hard-headedness. Does things right.	Lacks inspiration or the ability to activate others. Over-concern with getting things right.
Team worker	TW	Socially orientated, rather mild, sensitive.	An ability to respond to people and to situations, and to promote team spirit.	Indecisiveness at moments of crisis.
Completer finisher	CF	Painstaking, orderly, conscientious, anxious.	A capacity for follow-through. Perfectionism.	A tendency to worry about small things. A reluctance to 'let go'.

project can really help break the ice and immediately assist everyone in understanding individual working styles and preferences, thus helping to avoid misunderstandings and conflicts at a later date.

Important notes

1 As individuals we are all a million times more complex than any questionnaire, and we always need to apply the rule that any such instrument is a potential aide to recruiting people to roles and teams. The results of such questionnaires must also be combined with a full assessment of the individual's work experience, skills and record of achievement. You should never select anyone solely on the basis of a questionnaire.
2 It must be stressed that no one has a single preference. Belbin indicates that most people will have one to possibly three preferred styles. Whilst we may have some we frequently support that with back-up styles. It is this fact that gives most of us our flexibility. So we need to remember that someone's profile can change based on life and work experiences. Crude stereotyping is not a positive application of the work.

The project manager's preferences

As the project manager we have to think about the impact of our own preferences on how we might manage our teams. If a strong shaper, we may have to guard against being too driven and failing to listen to alternative views or ideas. As a resource investigator we would need to ensure that we stay focused and attend to issues of detail as well as building relationships with stakeholders or project sponsors. For the powerful plant there is a need to restrain his or her individualism and sometimes harsh and outspoken criticism of other people's ideas. An understanding of the various preferences helps us understand our own traits and how they need to be managed and combined with the technical aspects of project management control.

For people who lack the attention to detail and liking for accuracy and precision that so characterizes the completer finisher or monitor evaluator the planning tools outlined elsewhere in this book are designed to make up for this. By applying the guidelines and techniques you can ensure that you develop the necessary focus on detail.

One of the key applications of Belbin is to realize that it is not always possible to have the perfect match either for us or within a team. However, by recognizing the various gaps that might exist we have a means to manage them. If I know that I am not a strong chair or co-ordinator or that no one in the team has a high preference for being either a company worker or team worker then we have a basis by which we can begin to manage the discrepancy.

It is possible to allocate missing or limited roles to specific individuals who may have some leaning towards that preference, even if it is not too strong; someone who perhaps has the highest score. The responsibility to apply and enforce those attributes is then given to that person by the project manager and team for the duration of the project.

In other situations certain individuals or possibly the entire team might undertake some kind of specialist training.

A team tasked with coming up with new and radical ideas or changes but which is lacking strong plant or resource investigator types – both tend to be innovative and challenging in their thinking – might undergo some creative-thinking skills training.

As project managers we have recourse to other strategies such as organizing training or finding temporary specialist resources to help overcome any gaps in the team's profile.

Managing role issues and conflicts in the team

As well as trying to get the balance of the team right we will also need to be alert to the fact that individual conflict can break out amongst team members. Whilst we will address later and in more detail the problems associated with difficult people, Belbin's typology also helps provide either an early warning of possible conflict or a method to analyse existing interpersonal or style issues. Outlined below are some classic situations to watch out for.

The shaper-dominated team

Managing a team with lots of shapers is always going to be lively, particularly if the skill levels and other aspects of the individuals' professional background are high. Whilst shapers can make things happen and when energized accomplish much, they can be prone to outbursts of ego. Personal clashes and conflicts can, if unattended to, become common as people jockey for positions within the team. Such teams demand from the project manager a very strong chair role to arbitrate and pull the team above such difficulties. This may mean taking a very strong position even if it cuts across one or two people. Left unattended to themselves many shaper-dominated groups may implode. The message for the project manager is to have or very quickly acquire strong skills in managing meetings and conflict-type situations.

Shaper-dominated teams also need strong control to keep their enthusiasm and thrust for success getting the better of them. The presence of completer finisher and monitor evaluator types helps provide a very important counter balance to the infectious 'it's obviously going to work' approach.

The plant chairman or project sponsor

It could well be that as a project manager your project sponsor or steering committee chairman is a strong plant type. Given the critical nature of the role and the importance of the relationship between the project manager and the sponsor this can be a difficult situation to manage. Remembering that plants are stimulated by ideas and intellectual curiosity. They may well like asking, 'what if?' type questions. This means that in terms of keeping the project on track and attending to the technical aspects of project tracking and control you may have a problem stopping your sponsor going off in different directions.

Whilst in principle there is nothing wrong in becoming deeply interested in a radically different approach to tackling the problem halfway through a project's life cycle, if such behaviour is experienced throughout a project's duration it can be very disruptive. But this is a potential behaviour that some high plants are capable of displaying.

As the project manager you will need to ensure that you stay close to your sponsor and keep them advised of the project's status. If new and different options emerge you must first of all be prepared to allow some time to debate and explore the option. Plants do not like having their natural curiosity and intelligence dismissed. You should also think about the manner in which your colleagues introduce or present information at key meetings. A clumsily introduced topic or presentation may provide just the opportunity for your sponsor to become interested or excited and potentially disruptive for the next forty minutes.

Finally, if as a project manager you possess high plant tendencies you will probably already be aware of the need to exercise self-control. The key to success is to exploit the assets – radical, original and independent thinking, intelligence – but control the potential liabilities such as dismissing other people or sulking if the ideas are not accepted. The people management and relationship skills are often key to the plant succeeding in a project, and for that matter any management, role.

Shapers and plants

People with strong shaper and plant profiles both tend to be strong individuals. But in that sense any real similarity ends. The shaper has an immense inner drive to get things done. He or she can often focus in on one approach and apply all their skills and talents to pushing the matter to a conclusion. In doing so they can be dismissive of people who do not see the route to success as easily or quickly as they do.

In contrast plants possess a steady and even-paced approach. Not always the best at communicating with others they may appear wrapped up with their own thoughts. Yet they are capable of being strong-willed and immovable when excited about something. The radical or innovative nature of their ideas or the less than enthusiastic welcome for the shaper's approaches may prove very irritating. Equally the plant may well find the quickness, pushiness and possible jumping to conclusions of the shaper equally off-putting. The real problem lies in the ability of each to clash over approaches. Both types will cling to their views at the possible expense of others.

The project manager needs to be on the look-out for such tensions and again exert strong chair-type skills to deal with the potential conflict. Focusing on the fundamentals of the project and the specific goals or targets can help both types to adjust their sense of ownership to single approaches.

The missing completer finisher and monitor evaluator

So often in management teams people are not interested in matters of detail, preferring instead to moving forward regardless of any omissions. It is obvious that any project management team must have the skills or disciplines that are characterized by the completer finisher and monitor evaluator. Again the skills and techniques detailed in this book provide the necessary disciplines. The need is to keep on track, follow up on matters of detail and co-ordinate key project elements. Any project team that lacks these Belbin types must focus their efforts on ensuring the attributes and skills are either acquired by existing members or brought into the team. People who have scores that reflect a leaning towards these preferences should be given authority to exercise the perspectives.

Some final thoughts

As project managers we can help our colleagues become better team players by implementing some of the following actions:

- Help individuals get to know each other – build the team – work together, eat together, celebrate together and build the spirit.
- Be direct about what is expected from team members in terms of their performance and behaviour.
- Model how you expect team members to behave – show them that you value and respect them – live the words of teamworking.
- Consult with the team on all important matters.
- Provide feedback to people – focus on successes as well as areas for improvement.
- Set tasks that force people to work together and collaborate.
- Expose the team to other groups.
- Remain available to people to discuss issues.
- Set time aside to think about how is the team working together. Do not get trapped into focusing only on the task.

PROJECT STAGE 3: TEAM-BUILDING

6 Project stage 3: leading

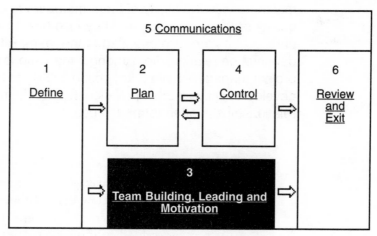

Figure 6.1   Team-building, leading and motivating

People chemistry is key – particularly on large and multi-team projects. As a project manager you have to be able to empathize with others. (Dennis O'Gorman, Senior Project Manager, Fitzpatrick Contractors)

Having looked at the development stages that a team goes through, the roles that people might play and the possible combinations of team composition we now need to examine the issues involved in managing and leading a project team. Leadership and management is a very complex and challenging process. No two situations are ever the same where people are involved and there can be no guarantees with regard to tools and techniques. But there is a large amount of practical advice and wisdom, that has its background in well-established theories, that can help us as project managers develop the right leadership style.

All management involves achieving the right balance between the task and people aspects of the role. On one hand we have to deliver the project on time and to the right performance criteria. To do this we also have to manage time and resources, the most complex of which is people. We not only have to manage stakeholders and the project sponsor but, critically, relationships within the team.

 Differences in teams are the reason a team can be creative, innovative and responsive. Such differences provide stimulation that increases the ability of team members to contribute to the quality of the team's output. They also help to ensure that different perspectives are also provided to the team. Effective teamworking depends on relationships amongst the various members and project managers have a key responsibility to help cultivate and develop effective working relationships. This management of relationships is often termed 'process'.

The critical project manager and sponsor relationship is another example of process. How that relationship works will depend on how well the two parties communicate and whether they have respect for each other. If one dominates, bullies or embarrasses the other, then the process will not be working effectively and the relationship will eventually flounder.

Where a manager fails effectively to manage the process either between a sponsor or project team they may experience any number of problems. A loss of commitment or productivity are just two. Although process may sound obscure it is in fact a complex set of behaviours and emotions that can be observed and felt by any team member.

Behaviours and emotions

Behaviours

- Who speaks and who does not?
- Who talks to whom?
- Who tracks time and action points?
- Who dominates and who gets interrupted?
- What sub-groups exist amongst the team?
- Who is serious and who is the joker?
- Who pushes the group forward?
- Who gets irritated?

Emotions

- How do people feel about working for the team?
- When is there an atmosphere of action, frustration, boredom, irritation, happiness and success?
- How does conflict break out? How is it dealt with?
- Does the team experience changes in feelings? How often do these occur?
- What causes the group to feel differently?

Managing process involves observing these behaviours and emotions and taking steps to ensure that they are managed effectively to help the group succeed. This means conflicts have to be dealt with rather than allowed to linger. Commitment has to be cultivated and maintained. Any project manager who is blind to process will invariably run into difficulties.

To begin managing the people-side of projects we have to start asking ourselves the following questions. The answers we receive will help us to begin thinking about whether or not we have the right focus and effort invested in managing the people and process side of projects.

- Do I enjoy managing other people?
- Am I able to get people moving and motivated?
- Do I encourage contributions and openness with other people?
- Do I value others' ideas and contributions?
- Can I manage conflict effectively?
- Can I make unpopular decisions?
- Can I deal with conflict effectively?

● Can I use humour and inject an element of fun into the team? How might other people describe my management style?

As regards the various tasks involved in leading a team, they comprise:

● *Planning the project* – setting out the path and goals; ensuring active team participation.
● *Organizing the team* – emphasizing team collaboration and involvement.
● *Setting team and individual goals* – these need to be realistic and stretching.
● *Delegating tasks and responsibilities* – this must be done in a clear and precise manner with appropriate authority given to the relevant team member.
● *Communicating* – employing a strong use of active listening skills and openness.
● *Managing conflict* – conflict should not be avoided but positively encouraged, explored and resolved.
● *Running meetings* – well planned, constructive and controlled.
● *Developing a working climate* – open, frank and positive.

Managing performance and setting team objectives

Good project managers must be good people managers.
(Paul L'Estrange, Manager – Development Support, Philip Morris)

To be effective any project manager is going to have to set individual objectives for team members. This process of individual objective-setting is normally termed 'performance management'. Setting objectives correctly requires the application of some basic rules. In the first case, managers have to be willing to invest time and effort at the start of a project not only to define the objectives but also to communicate them.

Too often problems arise in projects because parties were confused or unclear as to the precise requirements that they were expected to deliver. This is often the direct result of either a failure to set clear objectives or a breakdown in communication between the project manager and an individual team member. As project managers we must ensure that when we are assigning roles, responsibilities or tasks to people, they are absolutely clear as to what it is they are expected to deliver and the timescales involved.

So how do we go about informing the team exactly what requirements are expected of them? At the outset of a project we need to be clear on all the following dimensions.

Overall project objectives

- What is the background to the project?
- Why are we undertaking the work?
- What are we trying to achieve?
- What outcomes do we expect to deliver?
- How does the project fit into the wider scheme of organizational life?

Everyone on the team needs to have a clear view of the answers to these sorts of questions. They provide a clear context for people to work in and later can often be a reference source when projects stumble or start to lose focus. Constantly reminding everyone of the bigger picture helps a team stay focused.

Key responsibilities

- What roles will people be undertaking on the project?
- What responsibilities will the project manager undertake?
- How will workloads and tasks be allocated to individuals?

What do individual team members have to do in their roles? Produce plans, timetables, conduct research, write reports, liaise with others, order materials, manage others, contact others, attend meetings, make presentations, etc? Defining who is ultimately responsible for what is the bottom line.

Key result areas

What are the critical success factors that ultimately determine whether someone has succeeded in their role? As project managers we must be precise as to the key results areas of each team member. Key results areas might include:

- achieving financial or utilization targets
- people management
- project outcomes
- client or customer relationships
- technical expertise.

Individual objectives

By taking an individual's key result areas and breaking them down we are able to provide a clear set of targets or objectives for the individual to achieve.

The classic dimensions of any effective objective are that they should be smarta:

- **s**pecific
- **m**easurable
- **a**chievable
- **r**ealistic
- **t**imely
- **a**greed.

Performance standards

Standards are the performance objectives that you expect team members to achieve. Standards act as benchmarks and set clear expectations for the team. When standards are achieved people will know that things are going well. Certain standards you apply may be the same for every team member, for example, the timely and accurate completion of any project paperwork or procedures such as time sheets.

Methods of measuring performance

As a project manager we must have a suitable means by which we can measure the performance of individual team members. We need to be clear as to how we are going to be able to judge the performance of team members. Setting *smarta* objectives in the first place is obviously the main factor but we also need to ensure that we can obtain the relevant information to make the final assessment.

In managing the performance of people, we recognize that people have different strengths and weaknesses or capabilities. Any successful manager takes account of these differences and is able to then manage in such a way so as to get the best out of each person's potential. The most effective way of achieving this is to set the right objectives for each individual. To do this it is essential when setting objectives with team members that you pose two questions to yourself:

● How competent is the individual to complete the task that I am considering allocating to them?
● How committed and motivated is the individual to carry out the task?

In asking the first question you are forcing yourself to consider the quality of knowledge, skills and experience that your colleague has to complete the task. By posing the second question you are assessing the level of willingness or motivation the person has to complete the task. Remember that it is possible for someone to be capable of doing something but not motivated to do so. They might be bored with doing that kind of work or experiencing other non-job-related problems such as personal problems. Alternatively, they could be simply lacking in confidence even though you rate highly their ability to do the job.

The answers to these two questions help us to determine the level of control and relationship support we need to provide and the performance targets we need to set. Some simple guidelines are provided below for the various types:

● *Highly competent, motivated and committed people* – these team members will want stretching targets to challenge them. You can also afford to delegate heavily to them in the knowledge that they always deliver.
● *Committed and motivated – but not yet fully competent* – these individuals will require stretching targets. But beware of setting targets that are too high. You will need to provide guidance and be available to lend support. The provision of appropriate training may also be required. You may need to be directive and spell out very clearly what the person is required to do.
● *Competent but not committed* – if individuals are not committed to their jobs or objectives we need to find out why. The possible

reasons have been outlined above, but only by engaging the individual in some kind of discussion will we be able to find out what the problem is. By providing a mixture of coaching, counselling and confidence-raising we may be able to bring about commitment in such people.

- *Incompetent and uncommitted* – we need to be asking if these people are really suitable for inclusion on the project team?

A directive style is appropriate where people may be lacking in know-how but are well motivated. Remember this does not mean you have to be aggressive but that you simply need to be explicit in telling people what they have to do. This style is also appropriate when you are dealing with people who may be unwilling to do something. Unless you tell them to do it will not get done, so you need to be directive.

In contrast a participative management style is appropriate when you are dealing with strong levels of competence and motivation. Competent and motivated people require a more involving management style where you are seeking to develop and grow their competence even further. To exercise a directive approach would probably result in demotivating them.

Leading projects: what good project managers do

- Provide a clear sense of direction at all times.
- Display lots of energy, motivate people and push for results.
- Delegate work and refrain from trying to do everything.
- Follow matters through to a conclusion.
- Make themselves available to the team.
- Be realistic and flexible in their approach.
- Are able to take tough decisions and say 'No'.
- Create an environment of mutual trust and fun.
- Fight for their team members.
- Manage the politics and network.

Provide a clear sense of direction at all times

Effective project managers stay permanently focused on their Terms of Reference and the overall goals of a project. They constantly remind people of the end goals and results. They take almost every opportunity during informal and formal meetings to emphasize the goals and direction that the team needs to be pursuing. It is unlikely that when working for such a project manager someone might say, 'Sorry but what are we trying to achieve here?' In effective teams everyone is working on the same lines and towards the right goals. Clarity of purpose stays high.

Display lots of energy, motivate people and push for results

Motivating any person requires a degree of enthusiasm and energy. It is difficult to get other people excited or motivated if we ourselves feel lethargic and lacking in energy. Great project managers understand the need to infect people with enthusiasm in order to motivate. As such they will work hard at displaying behaviours that unite and enthuse the team. How do they do this? Well, for one thing they will physically display lots of energy. In meetings, for example, they might get up and down, walk around and use a flip chart a lot. They might pull people to one end of a table to show them something. Anything that displays energy or which gets other people to display it can help.

At the same time effective motivators use their voice to attract and stimulate people. Stating that a project is very interesting and exciting, and that you are pleased to have everyone working on it, but saying it in a very dull, subdued and monotone voice is hardly likely to motivate anyone. And that is the point, by simply using our voice tone more effectively we can get other people moving. By adding more power, tone and variation we can use it to energize others.

Delegate work and refrain from trying to do everything

On almost any project it is not possible for one person to do all the work. Effective project managers recognize this and make correct use of their ability to delegate tasks based on a proper assessment of individual's skills as outlined in the previous section. Project managers who are overly directive and controlling invariably run into difficulties with their more able performers. As such, good project managers know what is important and what needs their attention and what does not.

Follow matters through to a conclusion

One of the key messages of this book is that projects must have a conclusion. They must eventually die. Project managers that succeed have a restless desire to follow through. They are not happy letting things slip or fall behind. They do not avoid confronting difficult issues, setbacks or bad news. Their desire is to bring the project in on time with the TOR met. If you are relaxed or casual in your approach when targets are not achieved you will need to reframe your thinking in order to become a professional project manager.

Make themselves available to the team

The technical content of project management is intense and some project managers may feel more comfortable working with the details of Gantt charts and risk analysis. This maybe because they have a strong technical background and derive comfort from working in fields where a high degree of precision and accuracy can be applied. But, as we have already emphasized, the other critical component in managing projects involves people. Expressing a real and genuine interest in people and making time available to them is another characteristic of the excellent project manager. How many times have we have heard in organizations statements such as:

- 'I can never get hold of her to speak about the issue.'
- 'He's always somewhere else, meanwhile we have a problem and I can't do anything about it.'
- 'I always feel under pressure to get through the agenda as soon as possible – they always seems to be focusing on the next meeting.'

The problem in such cases is that the project manager is not devoting sufficient attention to the team. Again some of the control procedures we have detailed in this book, and in particular those in relations to project controls, should ensure that key meetings are held. But there is a difference between holding set meetings and conveying a sense that you are readily accessible and available to discuss problems or issues. So we need to work hard at making sure we do not just allocate time to people but that it is also quality time.

Be realistic and flexible in their approach

So far we have stressed the requirement for project managers to be very outcome oriented. We have to be results focused. For us not to be is to risk almost certain failure. But that does not mean that we have to be intransigent in our decision-making or management style. If genuine difficulties or obstacles emerge on a project then good managers react in a reasoned and mature manner. Throwing tantrums or getting angry with other people is the sign of a very disturbed manager. The experienced project manager knows that it is possible to maintain a powerful focus on results but combine it with a reasoned and flexible outlook in the face of changing circumstances.

Are able to take tough decisions and say 'No'

There are several times in any project when the pressure is on and the manager may be required to take a tough and difficult decision. It could involve confronting a sponsor over the failing of one of his or her people to deliver, or the need to abandon a big team investment in part of a project's work due to poor results. These moments are always difficult, but decisiveness is one of the characteristics of the great project manager. He or she knows when to make the break and is comfortable in taking swift action. Drawing difficulties out never works and only puts off problems until a later date.

Saying 'No' to people is often very hard for some of us. We may fear rejection or the possibility of a conflict or argument. Some of us are concerned that we might upset someone and this troubles us more than the person you may have to give the news to. Yet the fact is that you cannot manage any project without making decisions, and sometimes one of those decisions may involve telling someone that they cannot have something or do something. It is part of any management role and if we are not comfortable with it we will need to change our perspective so as to develop this essential skill.

If you are someone who struggles with this ability remember that you can actually say the word 'no' and that there is no physiological reason why you should be unable to utter the word. Indeed in our private lives we may readily use it all the time with our spouse, partner, children and relations. So often it is not the saying of the word that we fear but rather the imagined or perceived response or consequence. We may tell ourselves in advance that he may no longer like me or she will be upset. What we need to focus on is the outcome of not confronting the problem and stay focused on the project outcomes. That is not to say that we need to be rude or abrupt in saying 'No', but simply to recognize that by not doing so may have dire consequences for the project's future success.

Create an environment of mutual trust and fun

Creating a positive working atmosphere where mutual trust and co-operation are the norm are further attributes of any successful project manager. Too much work in most of today's organizations is gritty and uninspiring. Any great team, be it working in project management, new product development, production or sales will experience a powerful sense of team spirit. High trust levels and fun prevail as opposed to politics, posturing and game-playing.

Promoting some core values such as openness, honesty, respect and support will help. It is not enough for any manager to simply say the words, he or she must also live them in their day-to-day dealings with the team. You can begin doing this by setting certain ground rules for the team to observe in meetings. 'Everyone listens, only one person speaks at a time', 'It is acceptable to be critical as long as you offer a positive alternative' are some examples of ground rules that might be instilled into a team's way of working.

Fun is the other vital ingredient. Successful teams find time to celebrate and laugh. The excellent project manager makes sure that the team enjoys their work. They do not begrudge the small party at the end of a key milestone. One-off awards of thanks might be made for outstanding performance. Fun and laughter is made of mistakes as long as the learning has also taken place. A constant atmosphere of 'heads down and work, work, work' is likely to result in a depressed and demotivated team. So make sure time is found for fun.

Fight for their team members

The willingness of good project managers to be available to team members has already been emphasized but another important people management behaviour involves the willingness of the project manager to support, defend and even fight for their people if they get into difficulties with sponsors or other relevant parties. Some projects may involve difficult and contentious areas that upset existing arrangements. As a defensive reaction some parties may want to destabilize the project by criticizing or attacking certain team members on grounds that are not well founded. In such cases effective project managers will always rigorously defend and support their people, regardless of the power of the complainant or the issues at stake.

Such action is the mark of a strong manager who engenders the full loyalty and support of their team. Pandering to the defensive frustrations of discomfited or injured parties is not part of the project manager's role.

Manage the politics and network

In some organizations department 'functions' are getting in the way of 'projects', to the detriment of the project. For example, a department's policy may prevent a team member from travelling although the project budget has adequate funds. (Flavio De Rosa, Clinical Scientist, F. Hoffman La Roche)

If we reflect on the fact that most large organizations are political rather than rational organisms then as project managers we need to be able to manage a certain degree of politics. Some organizations are more political than others are. Survival in certain organizations may be largely dependent on a manager's ability to recognize the power plays and sources of influence that get things done. In managing projects we would suggest that a basic rule is for managers to stay clear of getting involved in any form of politics or intrigue. However, to do so would leave us open to the criticism of naivety.

There are a multitude of organizations where the only thing that matters is the results of the projects. In such companies people will talk openly and honestly. If aspects of a project are upsetting or potentially challenging to people the issues are dealt with in a mature and open manner. Deal-fixing and trade-offs whereby critical issues are lost or conveniently not raised do not apply. The danger with playing organizational politics is that it creates further complexities and problems. People may seek revenge or stall future developments for past acts.

So the basic rule is to try to avoid being a political animal and stay focused on the guiding principles that this book describes. There is no problem with a manager being aware of the various power structures that might exist in the organization and how he or she needs to manage the various levels of communications to keep the momentum and support necessary for a project. Indeed this is just good stakeholder management. But it is another issue actively to engage in subversive activities such as selectively leaking information or playing people off against each other to win over important points or progress matters.

Some people might argue that we should do whatever it takes, but experience suggests that organizations that have these negative political overtones and characteristics have bigger and deeper problems that eventually catch up with them. Stick to the fundamental principles of project reporting and control, and leave the games to the management neanderthals.

Networking, however is something that project managers do need to do, particularly in today's matrix-organized structures. In the digital-era company, it is no longer what you are that matters but what you know and can do. Knowing lots of people and where to get resources from can therefore be a huge asset to any project manager.

Unfortunately many people are not prepared consciously to think about and actively develop their network. In describing Belbin's work we highlighted the resource investigator type. These people are life's natural networkers; they can very quickly contact someone to try to secure help, advice or resource for a project. If you are someone who can readily recite an array of contacts, then, congratulations. If not, get yourself known in your organization.

You will never develop a network unless you personally work at it. Sitting in an office all day is not the way forward. Start thinking about volunteering or getting involved in areas outside of your normal daily work sphere. Write an article on a piece of work for your company newsletter or bulletin board. Be prepared to make presentations on your work or that of your department. Seek out people who have done interesting work and ask to speak to them about it.

Project leadership: a quick checklist of behaviours

Initiating the project's start-up

- Gain an understanding of the project's goals.
- Develop the initial Terms of Reference – make it achievable and realistic.
- Secure your sponsor's commitment.

- Sign off the TOR with the sponsor.
- Begin thinking about team's selection – skills and personalities.
- Select the team.
- Assemble the team.

Getting the project off the ground

- Introduce the team.
- Make them feel valued.
- Provide a clear set of project goals and outcomes.
- Match roles to skill sets.
- Discuss and agree clear objectives and responsibilities.
- Build a team spirit and identity.
- Produce a detailed project plan.
- Install agreed working methods and team procedures.
- Set standards in work methods and behaviours.

Project implementation

- Monitor progress against the plan.
- Communicate with the team, sponsors and other parties.
- Manage the sponsor relationships.
- Hold focused team meetings.
- Co-ordinate the team's activities.
- Deal with difficulties and setbacks.
- Celebrate successes.

Project review

- Review successes and areas for future improvement.
- Communicate the team's success to others.
- Celebrate success with the team.
- Extract the key learning and future action points from the project.
- Implement key learning into your future project management practices and methodologies.

Essential do nots for the project manager

- Ignore people.
- Try to do everything.
- Have favourites.
- Allow disagreements or conflicts to fester.

PROJECT STAGE 3: LEADING

- Stop listening.
- Be selfish and self-centred.
- Avoid problems or difficult issues.
- Be rude, aggressive or bullying.

Essential dos for the project manager

- Stay close to the team.
- Listen, listen, and listen.
- Set clear goals and objectives.
- Spend time reflecting on the process side of teams – how well are we working?
- Communicate with clarity.
- Catch people doing things well and congratulate them.
- Be sincere and genuine.
- Be consistent in all your dealings.

Managing projects: self-analysis

Understanding your areas of focus

Project management involves managing a complex set of competing and sometimes conflicting needs. The purpose of this questionnaire is to provide you with an indication of how effective your management style is in achieving a balance across these factors.

Work through the following statements and rate each in terms of how frequently that statement is true of your project management style. If the statement is the 'often' characteristic of your project management style, circle 2. If your response is only 'sometimes' true of your behaviour, circle 1. If the statement is 'rarely' characteristic of your project management style, circle 0.

Timing: The questionnaire will take you about ten minutes to complete.

Question	Often	Some-times	Rarely
1 I have reasonably easy access to senior management when I need to discuss issues affecting my projects	2	1	0
2 I can use a wide network of contacts throughout the organization to move my projects forward	2	1	0
3 I have good sources of feedback on the results achieved so far by my team	2	1	0
4 I feel confident that I can see the way a project will develop	2	1	0
5 Everybody in the project team knows exactly what is expected of him or her	2	1	0
6 I consciously try to develop and improve my leadership skills	2	1	0
7 I can discuss disagreements about the project with senior managers	2	1	0
8 I can persuade other departments to provide additional resources if I need them	2	1	0
9 The whole project team celebrates when we reach an important milestone	2	1	0
10 The project team is able to foresee and cope with problems and pitfalls on their own	2	1	0
11 I try to ensure that the whole project team meets throughout the project	2	1	0
12 I actively seek feedback from team members on my management style	2	1	0
13 I try to analyse the political and business implications of my project	2	1	0
14 I encourage team members to manage relationships with people outside the team	2	1	0
15 I try to share responsibility with the team members for keeping the project on track	2	1	0
16 I seek information on progress from team members and from other people	2	1	0
17 I analyse the personal and technical strengths and weaknesses of team members	2	1	0
18 I review and update the priorities and viability of the project	2	1	0
19 I try to identify all the stakeholders and analyse their needs throughout a project's life cycle	2	1	0
20 I consciously and actively sell the project throughout the organization	2	1	0
21 I deliberately take time out to anticipate problems and challenges for my projects	2	1	0
22 The project team does not repeat mistakes	2	1	0
23 I ensure the team is aware of the importance of the project to the business	2	1	0
24 I consciously sound confident when discussing the project with team members and others	2	1	0
25 I keep everybody fully informed throughout the life cycle of the project	2	1	0
26 I encourage the team to make key suppliers and people feel part of the team	2	1	0
27 When we face problems I expect the project team to take the necessary action to get it back on track without waiting for me to take all the decisions	2	1	0
28 I encourage the team to be fully involved in planning the project and anticipating problems	2	1	0
29 I work hard at developing team spirit amongst the project team	2	1	0
30 I have specific methods for dealing with my stress rather than allowing it to affect the project	2	1	0
31 When I am having difficulties on a project I feel I can go to senior management for help	2	1	0
32 Under pressure I can find ways to get things done informally in the organization	2	1	0
33 I ensure that team members and stakeholders know what we have achieved and where we are now	2	1	0
34 I have sufficient resources to achieve deadlines	2	1	0

Question	Often	Some-times	Rarely
35 I give team members regular and honest feedback	2	1	0
36 I make time to review our performance	2	1	0
37 Senior managers understand the contribution the project will make to their business	2	1	0
38 I try to involve my stakeholders in the project	2	1	0
39 We have effective systems for measuring progress	2	1	0
40 The project team hits its deadlines	2	1	0
41 I try to encourage the project team to try new things and to be creative	2	1	0
42 I ensure that all members of the team are kept fully informed	2	1	0

Enter your score for each statement in the appropriate numbered box below. Add up your scores in each column and enter the total for each in the total box provided.

1	2	3	4	5	6
7	8	9	10	11	12
13	14	15	16	17	18
19	20	21	22	23	24
25	26	27	28	29	30
31	32	33	34	35	36
37	38	39	40	41	42
A	B	C	D	E	F

Totals

What the scores reveal

The higher your score the more effort you are placing in the areas listed below. Areas that you score low in suggest that you should be devoting more time and effort to them in order to improve your effectiveness as a project manager.

A – Managing senior managers' expectations and meeting the business needs

B – Managing stakeholder relationships

C – Managing progress and reviewing achievements

D – Planning ahead and managing the future

E – Managing the project team

F – Self-management, managing and developing your individual effectiveness

Improvement actions

Managing senior managers' expectations and meeting the business needs

- Avoid getting too wrapped up in the technical aspects of the project.
- Stick to rigid reporting dates and keep your sponsor informed.
- Remind people of the terms of reference and the outputs from the project.
- Correct people if you hear the project being described in the wrong way.
- Stay alert to how the project relates to business performance.
- Sell and promote the benefits of the project to the business.

Managing stakeholder relationships

- Pay more attention to keeping close to your sponsor and other stakeholders.
- Ensure that you have regular meetings – informal as well as formal.
- Ask the sponsor and stakeholders what reactions they are getting from other people.
- Check out in detail the sponsor's reactions to progress.
- Give your sponsor ammunition to help them sell the benefits to other people.
- Do not become political but think about the organization's networks and what they might be reporting about the project.

Managing progress and reviewing achievements

- Stick to our recommendations on project control.
- Hold the regular project meetings – do not cancel.
- Ensure that the full team meets to review progress.
- Avoid the temptation of slippage or overrun – stay focused.

Planning ahead and managing the future

- Keep in front of you at all times the main aims of the project.
- Helicopter above the day-to-day detail and anticipate where the project is heading.
- Use lots of sources to check for problems or challenges to the project's success.
- Keep in close contact with all team members.
- Consider mistakes or errors and review them in the light of the project's long-term success.
- Be realistic – if a real problem has resulted in a need to reschedule do it! Do not try to fool people.

Managing the project team

- Question the amount of time you are allocating to individual team members – is it enough?
- Maintain daily contact with the team.
- Learn to distinguish between who needs technical help and who needs some moral and relationship support?
- Work alongside team members – ask to attend some of their meetings or presentations.
- Carry out regular individual reviews.
- Praise good performance both privately and publicly.
- Confront difficult issues.
- Provide opportunities for individual growth and development.

Self-management, managing and developing your individual effectiveness

- Take time out to reflect on your role and performance.
- Ask yourself if you are focusing on the right issues and priorities.
- Watch your time management.
- Concentrate on your successes.
- Learn from the mistakes but then forget about them – do not let them linger.

- Practise some stress management techniques – watch out for signs of stress.
- Take time out to recharge your batteries.
- Make sure you ask for feedback from others – the team, sponsors, senior management etc.
- Get some time away from the project – quality thinking time.

Stakeholder analysis

A key component of managing any project is the ability of the project manager to stay focused on the various stakeholders who may be involved in the project. Failing to manage stakeholders may ultimately lead to a disastrous project. It is critical that any project manager thinks about the various perspectives that different stakeholders may have on the project and manages the relationships.

One simple but powerful means of reviewing stakeholders' positions is what is called the 'power and concern matrix'. This process involves plotting the amount of power and concern a stakeholder may have on a project as shown in Figure 6.2.

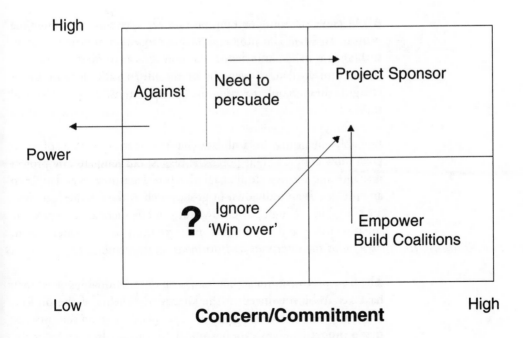

Figure 6.2   Managing stakeholders: power and concern matrix

Power is defined as the ability to get things done in the organization. Such people may have strong authority through the organization hierarchy or be seen an influential figures because of their technical knowledge. Concern is defined as the level of commitment that someone might have in making sure a project or its outcomes succeed.

Using the simple matrix in Figure 6.2 it is possible to map the various parties and their views on the project. This can be done using named individuals or groups or functions. The matrix is a flexible tool that can be amended to each individual project.

The benefit of such a matrix is that it enables a project manager to plan his or her tactics and to involve the sponsor in deciding critical actions. Any project requires a sponsor who is high power/concern – someone who is passionate and committed but also influential; a person that can get things done.

With stakeholders defined as high concern/low power the project manager may need to plan strategies to empower such people. Given the chance they will become advocates of the project. So tactics need to be developed to provide power to these individuals to support the work of the project and its aims.

A low power/concern ranking poses a big question mark over the people involved. The project manager can either choose to ignore such groups in the knowledge that they appear to matter very little to the project. Alternatively, he or she might seek to motivate or energize these people towards the project's aims, as an additional support.

Probably the most critical box on the matrix is that of high power/low concern. This poses the biggest challenge to any project manager and a failure to manage this box determines real danger to any project. If an individual or group, such as the finance function, are placed in the high power/low concern box there are two possible interpretations and any project manager must be very careful as to how he or she interprets and proceeds on this issue.

The first interpretation is that the group or individual involved may have yet to be convinced of the virtues or benefits of the project. They may believe that they have a better perspective on the issues or that a proper business case has not been set out. In such cases the project manager may need to redouble the communication efforts to this group or person. Perhaps they may want to co-opt the involvement of their chief sponsor to help the process, the aim being to shift this individual or group to a high power/high concern position. In certain high-profile projects such a shift could ultimately determine the success or failure of a project as it might be that too many high power/low concern groups or individuals may eventually scupper the overall project.

The second interpretation of this high power/low concern group is the negative one, namely, that they are ultimately against the project and at worst may wish it to fail altogether. Depending on the circumstances involved this could be become a very difficult and contentious project with people actually working against its stated aims. In such cases the project manager will need to provoke a crisis meeting with the sponsor to spell out the difficulties and implications for the project.

The power and concern matrix should be used at the outset of a project as well as throughout its life cycle. Being clear as to where stakeholders stand at the beginning of a project is critical but it is also possible that people lose interest or develop other priorities once a project is under way. The stakeholder analysis grid helps the project manager keep a close focus on the critical issues of commitment and support. It is a tool that can be used to supplement the tool kit of controls as well as being used in informal sessions with a project sponsor to highlight issues or concerns.

7 Project stage 3: motivitation

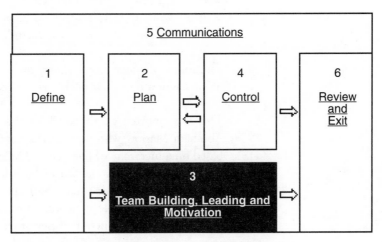

Figure 7.1 Team-building, leading and motivating

Convince the team that the success of the project is mutually beneficial for the company and that it is especially beneficial for them. (Alan Goodson, Project Leader, The Dow Chemical Company)

Motivation is what drives most human behaviour. Motivation is the engine that makes the vast majority of us commit to do specific things in life and it comes from within. There is no manager on Earth who can motivate someone who has already decided that they do not want to do something. Our motivational needs drive us to behave in certain ways in order to achieve specific goals. Understanding what motivates people helps us to explain and predict their behaviour.

The guideline for achieving success in motivating people on a project team, or for that matter any other human endeavour, is that first someone must be willing do something. The manager's role is to provide an environment in which motivated people can flourish. This in turn involves a manager being able to satisfy the following questions:

- Do I feel valued?
- Am I challenged and stimulated by my work?
- Is my work and success recognized and rewarded?
- Will I be able to grow and develop here?

The ability of a manager to satisfy these needs determines the degree of satisfaction that their people will feel in working on a project.

This is supported by the work of the world-famous psychologist Abraham Maslow who pioneered a particular theory of motivation based on a hierarchy of five needs. These begin with the satisfaction of physical needs and end with what Maslow termed 'self-actualization'. Maslow concluded that physical security, safety and affiliation needs motivate people to work, whereas self-actualization and the need for self-esteem encourage performance once people are at work.

Superior performance results from the need for self-actualization – the need to feel fulfilled. Indeed a central message of Maslow's work is that while the lower needs no longer motivate once they are fulfilled, self-actualization motivates to continually increasing levels of performance. Also it indicates that offering someone more money to work harder may be fruitless if they are seeking greater fulfilment. Instead you might need to offer more challenge or responsibility.

For someone to become self-actualized will require them to stretch their abilities. Where such a need is not spontaneous the project manager may need to create an environment to foster it. One way to do this is by establishing goals that push the person to achieve beyond their immediate grasp. The project team environment must value and emphasize outputs. At the same time, providing constant and accurate feedback on performance is another important element of creating the right motivational environment. Anything that provides a measurement on progress gives people the opportunity to assess how they are getting on. Listed below are some classic types of high-level motivators. As project managers we need to seek out opportunities to provide the opportunities for people to realize them.

● Sense of achievement.
● Recognition of ability.
● Interesting and challenging work.
● Responsibility.
● Promotion.
● Rewards – financial.

Of course it goes without saying that money is a motivator, as is a manager's attitude towards their staff, but often too much focus is paid to the impact of money. Whereas the evidence is clear that above a certain level money ceases to be a motivator to harder work. People also have different requirements as to what they might consider is enough money. Motivational theory also teaches us that it is not the money that people often work for but what the money provides that is the real motivator. For some people it might be independence; the opportunity to say goodbye to the company. For others it might be power; the ability to buy things that will impress other people.

To gain further insights into individual motivation we need to examine another approach.

The three basic motivators

Harvard University psychologist David McClelland developed a very useful theory of motivation that we can see and apply almost every day. His extensive work resulted in a theory that is based on people having three fundamental needs:

● the need for achievement
● the need for affiliation
● the need for power.

His work pointed out that we all possess these types of motivational needs but that we experience them to different degrees of intensity.

Whilst these needs exist alongside lots of other motivations they are viewed as being very deep seated and as a result cause us to behave in certain ways or patterns that can be predicted to some degree.

The practical application of McClelland's work is that people who have a high need for achievement motivation think in a particular way, just as affiliation and power motivated people do. Consequently, these thought patterns which are constantly running inside someone's mind eventually lead them to be behave in a certain way.

McClelland was able to codify these thought patterns and behaviours to produce a useful approach to help us understand other people and why they behave the way they do. For the project manager it is an approach to help understand:

● our own individual motivational pattern
● the motivational pattern of our team members
● the motivational pattern of our project sponsors.

By using the basic principles of McClelland's model we can quickly gain valuable insights in how best to manage and motivate team members as well as engaging in more productive working relationships with project stakeholders and sponsors. In using the approach the requirement is simply to focus on people's individual behaviours and statements in order to gauge signs of their motivational pattern. This does not require someone to become an amateur psychologist but merely to observe what is already in front of our eyes and ears.

But let us outline the three forms of motivation.

The need for achievement motivation

If the project is a success make sure all the team participate in its success – don't grab all the credit and limelight – people remember. (Dennis O'Gorman, Senior Project Manager, Fitzpatrick Contractors)

People who have a high need for achievement motivation are concerned about improving their performance and increasing their effectiveness and efficiency. They tend to do this by setting themselves very high internal standards of excellence, always looking to do the job better and improve on their last performance. They like to beat themselves rather than other people.

Highly achievement motivated people also like to exercise strong control over their work as they have the knowledge and confidence that they can succeed. Consequently they may like to work on tasks alone. They will also express a keen interest in and have an immense appetite for feedback on their performance. Indeed, one of the ways to irritate the highly achievement motivated person is to not provide any information on how they are doing. Interpersonally they often appear quite tough and even brusque. They want to get the job done and do not always worry about the other person's feelings.

The classic door-to-door sales role is a perfect example of an achievement motivated job. The individual is not managed, they are left to get on with it. They get instant feedback on their performance with every customer they meet. They have the opportunity to try out new and innovative sales approaches. They also earn in relation to the effort they put in. Their tough interpersonal shell means they can cope with the constant rejection and rebuffs from potential customers. So we can see how such a job would appeal to many highly achievement motivated people.

The need for affiliation motivation

Individuals with a high affiliation motivation are concerned with establishing close, friendly relationships with other people. Their concern is with maintaining positive relationships and avoiding any unnecessary break-up or fracturing of team spirit. Affiliation motivated people generally possess excellent interpersonal skills and are able to develop and nurture others. They tend to do well in positions that require them to help others or manage people to accomplish a task. Able to motivate and build team spirit they help a team function extremely well. Frequently they will know a great deal about their colleagues and be well liked and trusted.

Affiliation motivation is often important to people who find themselves either in repetitive work such as production working or, alternatively, stressful work such as customer care where their people skills can help relax irate customers. Affiliation motivation is also important in roles that require a lot of cross-functional relationships and communications. Research suggests these people also make great team leaders and supervisors.

The need for power motivation

People who have a high need for power motivation are interested in influencing and impacting on others in order to get things done. It is the motivation that is most associated with management. At best, power motivated people work for the good of everyone; at worst they can be selfish and egotistical.

Power motivated people tend to be very good at influencing others; some may even be charismatic. They often possess excellent inter-personal skills, and some are very good at reading the political agendas in organizations and are able to get others to work towards a common goal. Status is also very important to many power moti-vated people. As such they tend to be concerned with their image and reputation as these send messages to other people as to who they are and what power they have. Rank and authority will be of inter-est so think about job titles when trying to motivate such individu-als. Also involve them in important meetings where senior managers are involved. To make them feel even better ask them to make the presentation.

Table 7.1 is a summary of the characteristics of each type and the sorts of things to look out for and avoid when dealing with each time. But do remember the following points when applying the approach:

- *Listen to the things people talk about* – self, control, results, goals, people, friends, influence, control, direction, image, status? What do they like to focus on? – small talk or straight into business with no time-wasting? Remember, the words help us to focus on what someone possibly values, and if we know what they value we have a means to motivate them.
- *Watch out for the behaviours* – power motivated people are often very conscious of status. Are you required to conform to certain forms of protocol in dealing with someone? Do they like to always feel in control? Affiliation motivated people will want to get their team or others involved to develop consensus and com-mitment. They will want to get to know you as a person. Watching how someone behaves tells us what they value.
- *Check out the skills as well* – how someone thinks and is perhaps motivated is only one part of the equation, you must also con-sider a person's skill set. I might think like a power motivated person but lack the actual skills required to influence others, in which case I will fail before I begin! So assess the person's skills as well as his or her motivation.

● *Remember people are complicated and can be a mixture of different types of motivation* – as we have already warned in a preceding chapter do not use any theory to simplify your world. Motivation is a complex issue and whilst there are colleagues who you can immediately identify using McClelland's typology there are probably a lot more where it is more challenging to get a simple result. The reason is that people are complex. So use any approach towards understanding someone else with caution. If you have doubts try to check out your assumptions by asking some relevant questions.

Getting project sponsors on side

I once heard a person say, 'You know you are a project manager when your secretary brings you coffee every morning.' I knew I was doing something wrong, because back at my office, I don't have a coffee machine ... nor a secretary! (Gregoire Bouille, MIS Analyst – Methodology and Education, Philip Morris)

One of the critical issues in managing projects is to get your sponsor motivated. A very important initial step in this process is to get them thinking that you are an excellent person to be working with. If we take McClelland's theory we soon realize that different profiles result in different needs. By using some of the basic elements of his approach we can very quickly produce some guidelines to follow. We then have the opportunity to create greater rapport with our key customer.

How to manage the achievement motivated sponsor

This project relationship will work best when the sponsor is kept advised of all progress. So the application of agreed reporting requirements should ensure no major problems. But you will need to watch out for the sponsor possibly interfering. Remember achievement motivated people like to be in control and they are not always good at remaining relaxed when things have been delegated. The strong application of the detailed project reporting disciplines we have outlined should offset any normal antagonisms. But make sure you never leave this sponsor wondering what is happening.

Table 7.1   McClelland's theory of motivation – general overview

	Achievement motivated	Power motivated	Affiliation motivated
	The need to perform well at a particular task is concerned with:	The need for power to influence or impress others is concerned with:	The need to establish and maintain warm personal relationships is concerned with:
Clues to motivation	● Meeting or surpassing standards of excellence ● Making a significant and unique contribution ● Competing successfully with others ● Realizing personal career goals	● Having control of situations ● Control through position and circumstances to influence others ● Recognition through status/position ● Greater responsibility ● Building a reputation	● Being part of a group or team ● Being liked and accepted ● Being involved with others in the work situation ● Minimizing the degree of conflict
Actions to promote motivation	● Agreeing targets and measurable performance standards ● Review performance regularly ● Focus on results and contribution ● Focus on personal improvement and development ● Approach work in a systematic manner with plans to achieve goals	● Ask them for ideas and suggestions ● Let them present ideas ● Demonstrate how they have influenced the situation ● Give them credit for success ● Assign them a role and get that recognized by others ● Keep them informed of major issues	● Showing interest in their personal circumstances ● Sharing information with them ● Emphasizing the 'we' ● Establishing some social contact ● Recognition of their role within the team
Actions to avoid	● Being vague about desired results ● Sporadic and unstructured discussions ● Over-supervision ● Withholding the necessary authority to act ● Applying unnecessary controls ● Infrequent performance feedback	● Excluding them from your decision ● Restricting their access to senior levels of management ● Withholding of authority ● Being autocratic with them ● Neglecting to show respect for their position or them	● Being abrupt or cold in your dealing ● Irregular contact ● Physically isolating the person ● Restrictive communications flow ● Being overly critical of others

Also ensure that any meetings that you run are highly focused and efficient. Achievement motivated people like to get down to business quickly, avoiding any real social conversations. Expect dealings with them to be slightly cold and to the point.

Achievement motivated people tend to ask themselves if the people they are working with are capable. So you will need to be alert and on top of your subject in order to keep them placated. Show and demonstrate evidence of your expertise and skills to impress them.

How to manage the affiliation motivated sponsor

This type of sponsor is going to be concerned with your interest in them and their people. Watch out for lots of involvement clues. They will want a project to perhaps solicit many views from different groups of people. Be prepared to work hard at meeting these needs even if at times it creates additional workload. To the affiliation motivated sponsor it means a great deal and an early offer to include the team in discussions will help to cement the relationship.

Expect to be quizzed about who you are and what you do but realize that this will not just involve your technical competence. Remember that affiliation motivated people are essentially interested in people. So you may well have to share a little about your likes and dislikes, your interests outside work, hobbies etc. Responding to the genuine interest of the affiliation motivated sponsor will result in you building a strong rapport. A great danger is to be dismissive of an overly affiliation motivated response, but do realize that affiliation motivated people have very strong interpersonal detectors and can spot fakes. So stay genuine and sincere.

One possible danger area lies in the affiliation motivated person's desire for unity and harmony. Should problems arise on a project and people have to be confronted, you will need to manage the process very carefully. Whilst affiliation motivated people are capable of giving bad news or confronting difficult issues it is not something that they necessarily like doing. They may have to build up to the situation. For the project manager this could present difficulties if a project hits a critical phase and tough decisions need to be taken by the sponsor. So consider building the relationship early on so that you can give sound advice to your sponsor. If difficulties arise get them to focus on the wider impact of the problem and what is likely to happen if the issue is not dealt with.

How to manage the power motivated sponsor

The power motivated sponsor can be a complex individual. In McClelland's original work he described this as the most complex form of motivation. On one level the power motivated sponsor can be the ideal client or customer: considerate, reasonable, businesslike and easy to do business with. On another level the power motivated sponsor can be a very difficult political game player. At worst they have the capacity to be conniving, duplicitous and thoroughly nasty. What both share however is a good understanding of how to influence or manipulate other people.

Power motivated people get people on their side either by strength of personality and charisma or manipulation. If their motivation is used in a constructive way such people can be a great asset to a project manager. They are able to sell ideas and proposals to others and are skilful at working through the obstacles placed by others. To do so they might used previous contacts, alliances or even favours. In complex projects these influencing skills can be a great asset to any team.

Most power motivated sponsors will be concerned as to what it is you can do for them and their plans to climb the corporate ladder or deliver success via the project's goals. So pay due respect to their authority or expertise. A good ploy is to ask them to lend their expertise and experience – flattery is a great motivator to them – by chairing or leading another part of the project if their diary allows it. Be prepared to defer to them for advice and counsel. Above all, pay them respect and defer to them on important matters.

Motivation issues within the project team

As well as using McClelland's approach to manage sponsors we can equally apply the work to project team members. Gaining an understanding of their needs will enable us to manage them in a more effective way. Below are some suggested guidelines.

The achievement motivated team member

Set clear and stretching targets – these people work best when they are being pushed. Place responsibility and trust in them. Achievement motivated people do not like to have people looking over their shoulder. Make sure you provide lots of performance feedback. One very easy way to demotivate an achievement motivated person is not to give them feedback on their performance. Remember that feedback enables you to assess when you are succeeding or not and that is a primary driver of the achievement motivated person. Be prepared for this person to be coming up with lots of new and sometimes radical ways or solutions to fix problems. Whilst too many may be frustrating, recognize that the individual is trying to improve the situation by doing something that has not been done before.

The affiliation motivated team member

The affiliation motivated team member will be a strong and well-valued team member. They will display lots of interest in other team members and as such are great for developing team spirit and motivation. As a project manager ensure that you allocate time to this team member. With the right skills they have the ability to not only be an excellent and supportive team member but with their interpersonal skills and antennae they can play other influential roles. Affiliation motivated people have the capacity to get others to like them and can therefore play strong leadership roles. Equally they may be adept at persuading other parties to assist on parts of a project.

The one area to look out for is when the team is experiencing problems on performance and you require a highly affiliation motivated person to give bad news or confront someone about their work output. The issue for the affiliation individual is not that they cannot deal with these situations but rather that they may need some time to work up how they are going to deal with it. They will generally be unwilling to simply jump in and get it over with. Their concern for others means they will want to do it with a degree of care and sensitivity. In extreme cases it may well mean that they might try to avoid such tasks. So be prepared to be on hand to offer support and coaching to them if necessary.

The power motivated team member

The power motivated team member will be concerned with getting involved in the important and critical elements of the project. They may well want to take leadership or supervisory roles provided they have the skills. Power motivated people will be keen to attend important meetings where all the interested parties are present. If they have the skills they will be keen to take a role in presenting information to the project sponsor or other team members. At best they can be highly effective in supporting the project manager to take on supervisory roles and acting as a credible liaison figure with interested parties. Power motivated people can make good leaders and their influencing skills can help sell the benefits of a project to relevant parties. So be alert to using their abilities.

At worst the power motivated team member might want to run before they can walk. They could be too interested in trying to demonstrate their apparent higher abilities and skills rather than actually getting down to some basic tasks and disciplines. This can cause a strain for a project manager who is under pressure to get results. So it will be important to ensure that all team members are made aware of their responsibilities and key deliverables.

Identifying someone's motivational profile

Consider someone you work with in the course of your job or that you might have to work with on a project. It might be a potential team member or a project sponsor or stakeholder. Take a little time to reflect on their behaviour as you experience it? Think about how they operate and put themselves around the organization?

Using the scoring scale listed below score each of the statements that subsequently follows:

A – Not really true of them
B – Sometimes true of them
C – Often true of them
D – Always true of them

1 *They like to set realistic challenges and get things done quickly and efficiently. —*
2 *They tend to be non-assertive and warm. —*
3 *They enjoy a good debate and like competing with people. —*
4 *They are systematic in their approach to tasks. —*

5 They are efficient and like dealings to be to the point. —

6 They are visibly disturbed by indifference and avoid cool or cold people. —

7 They like to take the lead in situations. —

8 They like to have a high profile at work. —

9 They take great pride in a completed task or assignment. —

10 They are good at taking risks. —

11 They will quickly form an opinion and persuade others of its virtue. —

12 They are concerned about their status in the organization. —

13 They begin conversations with a non-business (e.g. social) discussion. —

14 They are actively concerned about the happiness and well-being of others at work. —

15 They volunteer for and pursue leading positions. —

16 They take every opportunity to present ideas/proposals to others. —

17 They actively plan their own development and career progression. —

18 They look forward to performance reviews with their managers. —

19 They actively seek the company of other people. —

20 They avoid conflict with others if possible. —

21 They work hard to keep conversations going and dislike silences. —

22 They enjoy recognition and publicity for their successes. —

23 They like to act as a representative or spokesperson for a group. —

24 They like to set measurable targets. —

25 They do not work well under close control or management. —

26. They work hard to create warm friendships and personal relationships. —

27 They tend to dominate conversations with their own views and opinions. —

28 They prefer to work in-group situations. —

29 They enjoy new learning situations. —

30 They show sympathy to those who are less fortunate or able. —

Identifying motivational factors

Transfer the ratings for each statement in the questionnaire (A, B, C and D) to the matrix below. The resulting total scores will provide a profile of the individual's motivation. Then plot the scores on the motivational profile matrix. Do not worry about absolute precision as you are only trying to get an approximate idea of where someone might be on the matrix.

Allocate the following scores: A = 1, B = 4, C = 6, D = 10

Achievement			*Affiliation*			*Power*		
Question no.	*Rating*	*Score*	*Question no.*	*Rating*	*Score*	*Question no.*	*Rating*	*Score*
1			2			3		
4			6			7		
5			13			8		
9			14			11		
10			19			12		
17			20			15		
18			21			16		
24			26			22		
25			28			23		
29			30			27		
Total score			Total score			Total score		

Motivational profile matrix

High (100)

Medium (50)

Low (0)

      n Achievement   n Affiliation   n Power

8 Project stage 4: control

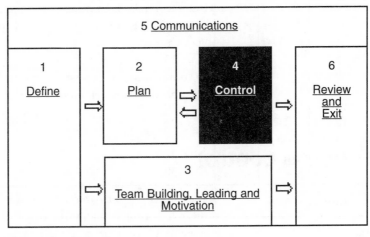

Figure 8.1 Control

Maintaining control

Do not let yourself lose focus. Regularly review your progress against the project plan (baseline) and focus, focus, focus, focus on reaching your goals. (Phillip Obraztsov, Regional Manager, Microsoft)

It is during this stage of a project that the majority of work is carried out by the team to meet the objectives. The project manager has to constantly keep the team focused on the deliverables and ensure that progress is tracked and reported on.

Maintaining control on a project has two very different aspects:

- process control
- environmental control.

Process control refers to the physical processes put in place to control the project. These include activities such as recording time sheets for tracking progress, preparing progress reports, managing change requests, holding reviews and replanning meetings. Process control needs to be enforced, and the rules for team discipline need to be clearly defined and understood.

Environmental control is about creating a working condition that makes the team feel that they own the project, understand the level of empowerment they have in making decisions, and a feeling of responsibility for delivering the project objectives.

The combination of process control and environmental control provides a balance between enforcement and encouragement.

Process control

Figure 8.2 gives an overview of the processes for controlling a project. The project plan is the baseline from which progress is measured and adjustments to the original plan are made. Clear rules on how information is gathered, and when control events take place need to be defined and then implemented. Each person involved in the project must understand their role and responsibility towards controlling the project. Each part of the control process will now be discussed.

Track progress

Have a good understanding of what your team members are currently doing and where they are with regard to the agreed deliverables. (Andreas Schmidt, Business Information Manager, Novartis)

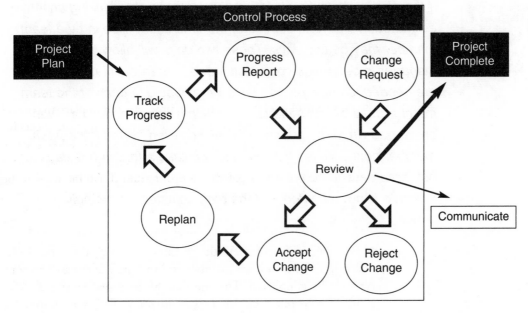

Figure 8.2 Overview of the project control process

Tracking progress is the first task that needs to be done to control a project. Regular reference to the project plan is necessary to control timescales, costs and the quality of deliverables. Timescales and costs are usually controlled by using time sheets, where team members record actual time spent on tasks. This actual time, or effort, spent on completing tasks will drive costs.

If the total time spent on a task called 'Interview in London' was five hours, then the cost can be determined by multiplying the resource rate with the time spent.

Time sheets are only part of the process of tracking task progress during a project. What the project manager must put in place is a method of asking each team member to confirm how long it will take to complete the remaining tasks. This is as important as asking them for the time they have already spent on a task.

If the plan records a task called 'Desk Research' requiring an estimated five days to complete, the time sheet filled in by a team member may be two days. These two days will allow the project manager to determine costs, but it does not follow that three days are needed to complete the task. What would happen, if the team member now believes the task is much more complex than was envisaged when the plan was initially created? What if the team member now believes that the task will take a further five days and not three days to complete? Project control is lost if the new estimate is not recorded and the plan adjusted accordingly.

New estimates to complete the remainder of each task need to be collected from each team member and the analysis matrix and time activity charts updated. The end date of the project may well have changed as a result of this new estimation. The most important factor here is that the information is collected and recorded so that the impact on the rest of the plan can be managed.

Progress reports

Watch out for early warning signs of a project in trouble: missed completion dates, poor quality, and requests for additional time, resources and funding. (Gabriel Williams RIBA, Managing Partner, Petersen Williams Architects)

While data from the team is collected to track progress of the project, a regular progress report needs to be prepared and circulated to the project sponsor. The same report could also be circulated to the steering committee members and team members. An example of a progress report can be seen in Chapter 9, Figure 9.8. At the top of the form is the usual information showing the project name, report date, project manager name, sponsor name and the list of people who will receive this report. These are followed by the budget section that compares the planned spending with the actual spend. Any request for additional budget is also recorded so that financial control of the project can be maintained by the sponsor.

Any unforeseen issues are reported in the issues section followed by a list of tasks that were completed. Any tasks that were not completed are then listed, together with a brief explanation. Finally, any new requirements or additional tasks are recorded.

Reviews and change control

In addition to tracking progress and preparing regular progress reports, a process must be put in place to control change. Quite often, this change process does not exist and changes are implemented without considering the impact on the plan. Referring to Figure 8.2, change requests need to be recorded and discussed at the regular review meeting. On small projects where there is no steering committee, the project manager presents the change requests to the sponsor, who then either accepts or rejects the change. The project manager then needs to update the analysis matrix and time activity charts. On larger projects, the steering committee together with the sponsor accepts or rejects the changes requested.

The process of managing change allows the sponsor to control the costs, timescales and quality of deliverables. On some projects, where significant numbers of change requests are made, a change control manager may be assigned the task of managing this process on behalf of the sponsor and steering committee.

An example of a change request form can be seen in Chapter 9, Figure 9.7. This form will act as a method for recording change requests and its main section describes the request and the benefit to the user and business.

The frequency of holding review meetings with the sponsor and steering committee during the control process is shown in Figure 8.3.

Replan

The final step in the project control process is to replan, that is, to update the analysis matrix and activity time charts. This updated plan is then communicated to the sponsor and team members.

PROJECT STAGE 4: CONTROL

Project Manager Meeting With:	Meeting Frequency
Sponsor	Between 2 to 4 weeks
Steering Committee	Between 3 to 5 weeks
Team Leader/Member	Weekly
User/Customer	Between 2 to 4 weeks
Suppliers	Monthly
Sub Project Manager	Weekly
Department Manager	Between 2 to 4 weeks

Figure 8.3   Frequency of meetings with project manager

Environmental control

 Have close contact with your team members and empower them as appropriate. Seriously consider the opinion of your team. Try to get the project (e.g. the scope and timetable) owned by the team. (Andreas Schmidt, Business Information Manager, Novartis)

Creating the right environment, or working conditions, where the team feels it owns and is responsible for the project is not created through force, but is created through encouragement, discussion and thought.

The project manager needs to know that the project management process, or methodology, is totally understood by the team, and that they 'buy into' this process. The team members need to understand everyone's roles and responsibilities, and why the project was commissioned. The first step in achieving these objectives is to present the terms of reference to the team and discuss people's roles and responsibilities.

These discussions can be followed by a short workshop where the team is asked to consider answers to the questions presented in

Control Factor	What happens in our organization?
Ownership 1. Does the team feel they own the project? Why? 2. Does everyone know who the project sponsor is?	
Empowerment 3. What authority does the team have to change objectives? 4. How can the team influence project progress?	
Team Participation 5. How does the team partici-pate in controlling progress? 6. How are progress team meet-ings organized?	
Measurement 7. How is project progress mea-sured? 8. Is there a better way to measure progress?	

Figure 8.4 Environmental control of a project

Figure 8.4. The discussion that these and similar questions generate will provide the answers the project manager needs to create the right environment for controlling the project.

9 Project stage 5: communications

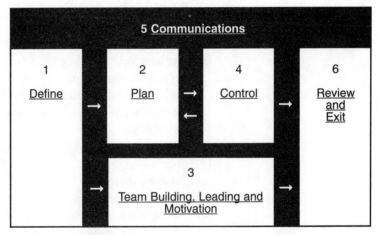

Figure 9.1 Communications

Keep relevant people in the picture about project progress, problems and plans. Liaise informally or report formally, as appropriate for the people, organization and culture – but do so regularly if possible. (Dalim Basu, Project Manager, ITN)

Communication is a critical process required for managing a project. The production, storage and distribution of information needs to be defined at the beginning of a project and effectively managed throughout its life. The responsibility for achieving this rests with the project manager.

Communication templates

Throughout this book we have made many references to using a number of forms to assist you in the process of recording and communicating information when managing a project. On the following pages we have outlined a series of templates that you might like to use or adapt to help you communicate effectively. They cover the key stages of our project management process:

1 Define
  (a) Sponsor meeting – Figure 9.2
  (b) Terms of reference – Figure 9.3
2 Plan
  (a) Analysis matrix: work breakdown, resource, effort/duration and cost – Figure 9.4
  (b) Analysis matrix: task schedule and project duration – Figure 9.5
3 Control
  (a) Actual cost versus budget tracking – Figure 9.6
  (b) Change request – Figure 9.7
  (c) Project manager's progress report – Figure 9.8
  (d) Problem identification – Figure 9.9
  (e) Request for additional improvements – Figure 9.10
4 Review and exit
  (a) Project manager's performance assessment – Figure 9.11
  (b) Sponsor satisfaction of project – Figure 9.12
  (c) Project manager's self-assessment – Figure 9.13
  (d) Project review – Figure 9.14
  (e) New system operation review – Figure 9.15
  (f) New process review – Figure 9.16
  (g) Additional notes – Figure 9.17.

Project definition – SPONSOR MEETING	
Date/Time	Address
Present – Name/Dept	
Meeting purpose	
What is the sponsor's reporting structure?	
Description of sponsor's operation	

Figure 9.2 Sponsor meeting

What are your sponsor's issues?	
What are possible project objectives?	
Initial thoughts to solve problem	
Action to take	
Next meeting date/time/place	Duration of meeting

Figure 9.2 (*continued*)

Project definition – TERMS OF REFERENCE

Sponsor name	Date
Project manager name	Location
Project title	Start date

Background

Objectives

Benefits to business

Figure 9.3   Terms of reference

Scope/Boundary of work
Constraints to be confirmed
Assumptions to be confirmed
Project reporting method
Deliverables and milestones (target dates)

Figure 9.3 (*continued*)

Activity Time Chart For Project:

Activity	Who	Effort	Start	Week 1 2 3 4 5 6 7 8

Total Effort: days

Estimated Costs
Resource Name: Rate: Effort: Cost:
Resource Name: Rate: Effort: Cost:
Resource Name: Rate: Effort: Cost:
Resource Name: Rate: Effort: Cost:

Equipment Name: Cost:

Expenses: Cost:
Expenses: Cost:

                        Total Estimated Costs:
£119,000

Approval

Sponsor Name:_____ Department: _____

Signature:_____ Date: _____

Figure 9.3   (*continued*)

PROJECT STAGE 5: COMMUNICATIONS

NEW SKILLS PORTFOLIO

Sheet No: of	Project Title:

ID	Description	Wk/Day/Hr	Month/Wk/Day																																	

Figure 9.4 Analysis matrix: work breakdown, resource, effort/duration and cost

Sheet No: of	Project Title:																	

Resource name and rate/day: A:-   B =   C =   D =

ID	Description	Depend	Effort A	Effort B	Effort C	Effort D	Duration	Cost A	Cost B	Cost C	Cost D	Total Cost	Probability of Failure H/L/M	Impact on project H/L/M	Contingency Action (If M/M or above)
												120,000				

Figure 9.5 Analysis matrix: task schedule and project duration

PROJECT STAGE 5: COMMUNICATIONS

Resource Expenditure

Resource Names/Rate:	A =	B =		C =		D =			
ID Description	Actual Effort A	Actual Effort B	Actual Effort C	Actual Effort D	Actual Cost A	Actual Cost B	Actual Cost C	Actual Cost D	Total Actual Cost	Budget	Variance (Budget Variance)

Invoiced Expenditure

Item Description	Amount	Budget	Variance
Totals			

Expenses

Item Description	Amount	Budget	Variance
Totals			

Figure 9.6 Actual cost versus budget tracking

Control – CHANGE REQUEST	
Requester name	Circulate to
Approved by name	Date

Describe the change you want made to the new procedure or system?

Why do you want to make this change?

How will this change help you do your job better?

How will this change help the business?

Date scheduled:	Date completed:

Figure 9.7   Change request

Control – PROJECT MANAGER'S PROGRESS REPORT	
Project name Report date	Circulate to *Implementation committee* *Sponsor*
Project manager name	Sponsor name
Budget *Project budget:* _____ *Actual spend to date:* _____ *Budget to date:* _____ *Variance to date:* _____	Reasons for addition budget
Issues	
Tasks complete	

Tasks not complete
   Reason:
   Reason:
   Reason:	

New additional requirements/tasks identified	
Staff absences:	Date next report due:

Figure 9.8   Project manager's progress report

Control – PROBLEM IDENTIFICATION

Interviewee name	Location
Assessor name	Date

Project name

What problems did you encounter while the new system/procedure was being developed and how were they resolved?

Immediately after the new procedures were put in place I think ...

Most people were advised of the changes:	Yes ☐ n/a ☐ No ☐
I knew who to see if there were problems with the changes:	Yes ☐ n/a ☐ No ☐
The benefits of the new procedures were explained:	Yes ☐ n/a ☐ No ☐
The transition to the new procedures went smoothly:	Yes ☐ n/a ☐ No ☐

Immediately after the IT system was put in place I think ...

The help line was easy to contact:	Yes ☐ n/a ☐ No ☐
Most of my problems were quickly solved by the help line:	Yes ☐ n/a ☐ No ☐
When things went wrong, I got help quickly:	Yes ☐ n/a ☐ No ☐
I could rely on the new system:	Yes ☐ n/a ☐ No ☐
I was given sufficient training to use the new system:	Yes ☐ n/a ☐ No ☐

Figure 9.9   Problem identification

PROJECT STAGE 5: COMMUNICATIONS

Control – REQUEST FOR ADDITIONAL IMPROVEMENTS

Requester name	Location
Approved by name	Date

Describe the change you want made to the new procedure or system?

Why do you want to make this change?

How will this change help you do your job better?

How will this change help the business?

Date scheduled:	Date completed:

Figure 9.10 Request for additional improvements

Review and exit – PROJECT MANAGER'S PERFORMANCE ASSESSMENT

Assessor name	Location
Project manager name	Date
Project name	

How much has the project manager contributed to meeting the following project objectives?

1	A lot ☐	Some ☐	Little ☐
2	A lot ☐	Some ☐	Little ☐
3	A lot ☐	Some ☐	Little ☐
4	A lot ☐	Some ☐	Little ☐

What specific actions did the project manager take to meet these objectives?

What did you like about the project manager's method of operating?

What did you dislike about the project manager's method of operating?

Did the project manager control the assignment to keep it ...

On time:	Yes ☐	No ☐	Why? ☐
In budget:	Yes ☐	No ☐	Why? ☐
To quality:	Yes ☐	No ☐	Why? ☐

I think ...

I would use this project manager again:	Yes ☐	Possibly ☐	No ☐
The project manager left valuable skills in the company:	Yes ☐	Possibly ☐	No ☐
I would recommend this project manager:	Yes ☐	Possibly ☐	No ☐
The project manager has significantly helped me:	Yes ☐	Possibly ☐	No ☐
The project manager worked well with my team:	Yes ☐	Possibly ☐	No ☐

Figure 9.11   Project manager's performance assessment

PROJECT STAGE 5: COMMUNICATIONS

Review and exit – SPONSOR SATISFACTION OF PROJECT	
Sponsor name	Location
Assessor name	Date
Project name	

What new benefits has the project given you?

What benefits should have been delivered?

What did you like during the development of the project ?

What didn't you like during the development of the project?

Was the assignment effectively controlled to keep it ...
On time: Yes ☐   No ☐   Why? ☐
In budget: Yes ☐   No ☐   Why? ☐
To quality: Yes ☐   No ☐   Why? ☐

I think ...
The new system/procedure is easy to use: Yes ☐ n/a ☐ No ☐
My role is easier to conduct using the new system: Yes ☐ n/a ☐ No ☐
The project manager involved me during development: Yes ☐ n/a ☐ No ☐
The project manager kept me well informed: Yes ☐ n/a ☐ No ☐
The documentation for the system/procedure is good: Yes ☐ n/a ☐ No ☐

Figure 9.12   Sponsor satisfaction of project

Review and exit – PROJECT MANAGER'S SELF-ASSESSMENT	
Consultant name	Date
Project name	

Have the following project objectives been achieved?

Fully ☐   Partially ☐   Not ☐
Fully ☐   Partially ☐   Not ☐
Fully ☐   Partially ☐   Not ☐
Fully ☐   Partially ☐   Not ☐

Why have objectives NOT been achieved?

What could I have done differently to improve the final result?

Was the project completed ...
On time: Yes ☐   No ☐   Why? ☐
In budget: Yes ☐   No ☐   Why? ☐

I think at the end of the project ...

My sponsor relationship is:	Good ☐ Fair ☐ Poor ☐
My relationship with the sponsor's staff is:	Good ☐ Fair ☐ Poor ☐
The team rate my work as:	Good ☐ Fair ☐ Poor ☐
My sponsor rates my work as:	Good ☐ Fair ☐ Poor ☐
My sponsor rates my project management skills as:	Good ☐ Fair ☐ Poor ☐

Figure 9.13   Project manager's self-assessment

Review and exit – PROJECT REVIEW	
Interviewee name	Location
Assessor name	Date
Project name	

What were the best practices in this project that we should use in future?

What should we avoid doing in future projects?

What groups were helpful during this project and how?

What groups were NOT helpful during this project and how?

Figure 9.14   Project review

Review and exit – NEW SYSTEM OPERATION REVIEW

Interviewee name	Location
Assessor name	Date

Project name

What do you like about the way the new system operates?

What don't you like about the way the new system operates?

Now that the system has been in place for a while, I think ...

The help line is easy to contact:	Yes ☐	n/a ☐	No ☐
Most of my problems are quickly solved by the help line:	Yes ☐	n/a ☐	No ☐
When things go wrong, I get help quickly:	Yes ☐	n/a ☐	No ☐
I rarely need to use help documentation or on-line help :	Yes ☐	n/a ☐	No ☐
I can rely on the new system:	Yes ☐	n/a ☐	No ☐
The information stored on the system is secure:	Yes ☐	n/a ☐	No ☐
The system is easy to use:	Yes ☐	n/a ☐	No ☐
The system responds fast enough :	Yes ☐	n/a ☐	No ☐

Figure 9.15　New system operation review

PROJECT STAGE 5: COMMUNICATIONS

Review and exit – **NEW PROCESS REVIEW**	
Interviewee name	Location
Assessor name	Date
Project name	
Describe the new procedure	
What you like about the new procedure?	
What DON'T you like about the new procedure?	

Now that the new procedure has been in place for a while, I think ...

The benefits of the new procedure are clear:	Yes ☐	n/a ☐	No ☐
The new procedure directly affects me:	Yes ☐	n/a ☐	No ☐
My role is now easier to carry out :	Yes ☐	n/a ☐	No ☐
The team I work with approve of the new procedure:	Yes ☐	n/a ☐	No ☐

Figure 9.16   New process review

Additional notes

Subject	Date

Notes

Figure 9.17 Additional notes

10 Project stage 6: review and exit

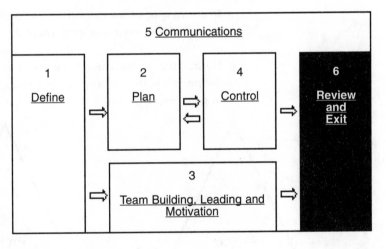

Figure 10.1   Review and exit

Why review a project?

The information we learn about our own performance and the process used to implement the project will provide valuable information to improve our performance on future projects.

Signalling the end

Take time out to celebrate and enjoy the success of a project before moving on to the next one. (Gabriel Williams RIBA, Managing Partner, Petersen Williams Architects)

A critical action at the end of any project is to ensure that your project's completion is formally agreed and 'signed off' by your sponsor. It is important to let your sponsor and steering committee know that the project has formally ended and been handed over to the user for the operational phase. Your sponsor will also know that any additional work will be subject to new terms of reference.

Completing a project is achieved by using your original TOR and presenting your sponsor with a report that will include:

- a review of various aspects of the project
- A review of your own performance.

Figure 10.2 presents an overview of this process. The complexity of the project will determine the amount of detail you need to present in your review report.

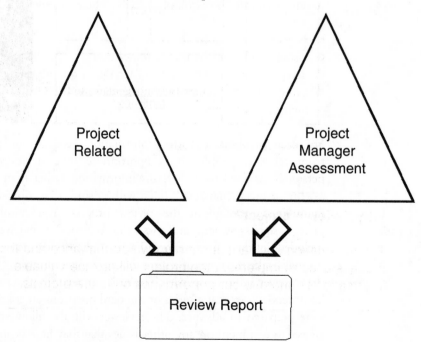

Figure 10.2 The review process

The benefits of using this process to sign off a project are:

- having a structured method for conducting your review
- getting feedback on your contribution and performance
- measuring the effectiveness of your work and the success of the project's results.

The review process

The two parts of your review process dealing with your own assessment and the project assessment, can be divided into a number of specific activities. These are presented in Figure 10.3, which shows that more effort must be directed towards the activities at the bottom of each triangle. As a minimum, you should carry out the top four activities, which are:

- a self-assessment
- assessment of you by your sponsor
- the effectiveness of the project
- the effectiveness of the planning and implementation process.

The other activities should be carried out if you have the required resources and funds to complete them. These include:

- assessment of you by the project team
- assessment of you by the customer/user
- determining customer/user satisfaction of the project
- gathering requests and recommendations for further improvements and changes.

For each of these activities, information needs to be gathered from relevant people. It is appropriate that an independent person is assigned to gather this information rather than yourself as the project manager. This will ensure that objectivity is maintained throughout the review process. You should complete a self-assessment and pass this on to the reviewer to be included in their final report. Each of the review activities will normally take the form of a series of one-to-one interviews between the reviewer and other parties. The reviewer needs to structure his or her interviews so that a series of standard questions are asked which were prepared in advance. The reviewer will also allow any interviewee to comment on any other issues that may have been missed. A questionnaire can be sent out to a variety of people to obtain their

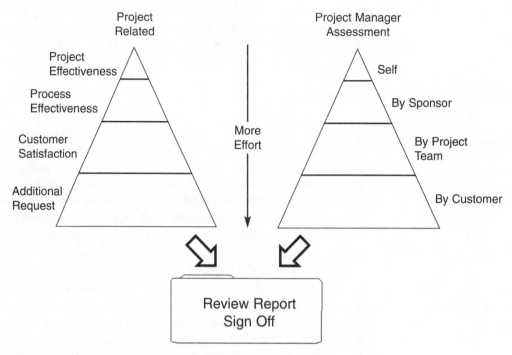

Figure 10.3 The review process in detail

views but more information will be obtained on a one-to-one basis.

To carry out a review the reviewer will need to:

- plan what information to gather
- conduct their interviews
- present the review report to the sponsor.

Planning what information to gather

A successful review will need careful planning as there are a number of steps that need to be carried out:

- Who should be interviewed?
- Prepare questions for the interviews.
- Arrange interview appointments.
- Prepare the review report.

The review process should be completed within one month. This should include carrying out the interviews, documenting them, analysing results, preparing a report and presenting this back to the project sponsor.

Who should be interviewed?

The type of project you have carried out will govern the answer to this question and the amount of time the reviewer has to devote to the review process. For example, if you were project managing the launch of a new IT system to a number of different organization sites, the reviewer might aim to interview a representative sample of users of the new system, the team who built it and information providers. Where applicable, the review should also extend to members of the steering committee and any departments that may have been supporting the project. This might potentially involve at least seven meetings and several more depending on the number of interviewees involved from each interested group. If there were several hundred final users of the system, the reviewer would probably want to select a small group of users representing a geographical area, be it nationally or internationally. Departments who provide regular information to the new system such as personnel, marketing, financial control, customer services and production might also be included. The people who built the system, the system developers, might include a mixture of both internal and external resource and again the reviewer would probably want to check their views. So very quickly the review process might include between twenty and thirty interviews that need to be completed. On very large and complex projects involving high levels of expenditure and large operational changes, the reviewer may well be required to carry out this size of review as the sponsor and steering committee will be looking to identify tangible results.

Conversely if you were responsible for organizing an annual management forum then the number of interviews would be significantly less. But even in this case the reviewer should aim to interview a cross-section of delegates, the sponsor and a representative sample of any external parties who may have participated in the conference.

Will your sponsor sanction a budget to carry out a review? On large-scale projects there will probably be a strong expectation that a full review will take place, but you may need to work hard at persuading your sponsor to fund a review on smaller projects. Much will depend on the circumstances surrounding the original project and the availability of a reviewer who may need to conduct a review in his or her

PROJECT STAGE 6: REVIEW AND EXIT

own time commitment. Where sponsor assistance is not forthcoming avoid the temptation to forget about a review, as they are vital to your improving your efficiency of running future projects. At the same time do not miss this important opportunity to document and sell the impact of your work.

Preparing questions for an interview

A range of questions is presented in this chapter for the reviewer to consider and use when structuring their review. Alternatively, the forms in Chapter 9 can be used to conduct reviews. The appropriate form can be used for the type of information that will be gathered according to the model presented in Figure 10.3. These forms include the following.

Project manager's assessment

- *Self* – project manager's self-assessment form (Figure 9.13)
- *By sponsor* – project manager's performance assessment form (Figure 9.11)
- *By project team or customer* – project manager's performance assessment form (Figure 9.11).

Project related

- *Project effectiveness* – project review form (Figure 9.14) or sponsor satisfaction of project form (Figure 9.12)
- *Process effectiveness* (IT system) – new system operation review form (Figure 9.15)
- *Process effectiveness* – new process review form (Figure 9.16)
- *Customer satisfaction* – new process review (Figure 9.16) or new system operation review form (Figure 9.15)
- *Additional requests* – problem identification form (Figure 9.9)
- *Additional requests* – request for additional improvements form (Figure 9.10).

Arranging interview appointments

After the reviewer has identified the people that need to be interviewed, appointments are arranged through your sponsor's office. The reviewer needs to find out where the people to be interviewed are located and to make allowances for travelling to their offices. If they are located abroad, provision needs to be made for obtaining any necessary travel approvals. As an alternative, it may be easier to ask if they would be willing to travel to the reviewer's office or your sponsor's office. Finally, if most people are located in one building, the reviewer must not be tempted into interviewing too many people in one day. His or her capacity to remain alert and focused will diminish as the day progresses. The reviewer should plan for a maximum of four or five interviews a day lasting about one hour each and having about half an hour between interviews to make final notes or to prepare before the next interview.

Planning the review report

At this stage enough time must be allocated to prepare the final report. The reviewer will now have a good idea of who to interview and should allocate at least two hours per person for writing up interview notes.

Conducting interviews

Always go into any review meeting extremely well prepared. Think carefully beforehand about the type of questions that you will want to ask. Use the forms presented in Chapter 9 to assist you in the process.

When the interview begins, make sure you inform the interviewee that your review is intended to measure the impact of your work and that they are not being assessed in any way. Relax the interviewee by discussing the background to the project, your involvement and who your sponsor is. Let them know that your sponsor will be circulating the review report to all those who participated in it. Before you begin with your questions, let them know that you will be noting down their responses. Do not hide your notes, and tell the interviewee that they can inspect them at any time during the interview.

Third party reviews

You need to be aware that you may not be the only person carrying out a review as your sponsor may want an independent third party to conduct an assessment. If another person, either within the organization or from outside, has been asked to carry out a review, you need to meet and discuss his or her structure for conducting the review. If you are also going to carry out a review, try between you to avoid interviewing the same people twice. Your credibility, and possibly that of the project, may suffer from this needless duplication. If two reviews are being conducted, discuss the aims and questions of you both. Understand the background from the other person's point of view and try to agree a joint timetable for interviewing and completing both reviews so as to minimize disruption.

Evaluating your performance

As a project manager you need to know which aspects of your assistance have been successful or not. You must validate the impact of your project management efforts. You also need to identify to what extent other organizational factors have influenced the outcomes of the project? Without this information, neither you nor your sponsor will be clear about how to manage similar situations in the future.

Assessing your own performance

Here are a list of questions you can ask yourself in order to assess your own performance on a project. You do not need to answer them all but use those most appropriate for the project you were working on:

- Were the project objectives achieved?
- Has your sponsor's problem been solved or addressed?
- What could you have done differently to improve the final result?
- What do your colleagues feel about the results of the project?
- How does your sponsor's staff regard your involvement?
- How good is your current sponsor relationship?
- Will your sponsor recommend you to their colleagues?
- Has your sponsor asked you to undertake additional work?
- Did the project stay within budget?

Other people's assessment of your performance

You also need to understand how other people and groups that participated in the project regarded your performance. Remember, you can ask this same set of questions to a cross-section of people who were actively involved in the project:

- To what extent do you think the project manager contributed to meeting the project objectives?
- What specific actions taken by the project manager helped to meet the project objectives?
- What specific actions taken by the project manager hindered you in meeting the project objectives?
- What might the project manager have done (but did not) that might have helped you to meet the project objectives?
- Would you use the project manager to help you address a similar situation in the future?
- Would you choose to work with the project manager again in the future?
- Would you recommend the project manager to colleagues?

Assessing customer satisfaction with a new system

If your project has resulted in a new system being implemented, such as a new accounting system, then you need to assess peoples' satisfaction with the new changes and the way they were implemented. You may identify two groups of people, for example, those that are involved in operating the new system and those that receive information from it. You might arrange to interview one person who will represent the views of each group. In many cases, you may have to interview several people from each group to obtain a balanced view. This process is usual when the project has involved people from different departments, such as marketing, production or human resource. All these people may derive benefit from or use the new system but they may have very different views on its effectiveness. You are looking to assess their satisfaction in either using or obtaining information from the new system.

Consider using some of the following questions:

- Has the system delivered new benefits to the people who use it?
- Have all the expected benefits been achieved?
- Is the new system easy to operate?
- Are jobs easier to do with the new system?
- Have the business objectives been met?
- Did the project manager involve people sufficiently during the project?
- Did the project manager keep people informed of progress?
- Is the documentation supporting the new system satisfactory?

Reviewing a new system or procedure

In some cases you will also want to determine the effectiveness of any new system or procedures. Here are some questions you may ask if a new procedure has been implemented such as a new ordering process:

- Have the original problems been addressed?
- What do you like about the new procedures and why?
- What don't you like about the new procedure and why?
- Will this new process make your job easier to do?
- Is the procedure quicker than the previous one?

For a new systems implementation, such as a sales monitoring system, you might use the following questions:

- Is the system easy to use?
- Are the response times fast enough?
- What do you like about the new system and why?
- What don't you like about the new system and why?
- If things go wrong, is there a contingency procedure?
- If the contingency procedure was used, was it effective?
- If information is stored on the new system, is it secure?

Identifying continuing problem areas

You may also need to identify any continuing problems being experienced by people as a result of the implementation. Here are a few questions you might ask:

- Have you had any further problems since the work was implemented?
- When did they start to occur?
- What do you feel is contributing to these problems?
- What actions have you so far taken to address these issues?
- Have you reported these problems to anyone else?
- Do you have any thoughts as to how the problem might be dealt with?

Reviewing your project process

In any project you should aim to review your project management process. This will help you and your sponsor identify successful practices and improvements for any future projects. So consider using the following questions:

- What practices helped to make the project go smoothly?
- What should we avoid doing during future projects?
- What difficulties did you encounter whilst the work was being carried out?
- What did you like about the work plan?
- What else helped to make the project run smoothly?
- Why do you think we had that problem with x?
- What other groups do you think assisted the development of the project?
- What groups or departments hindered development?

Gathering recommendations for additional improvements

Although a new system may have only been in place for a short time before you carry out your review, it is none the less likely that requests for further changes will be made. Apart from recording these requested changes, your review report can also impress on your sponsor the need for a process to manage these requests for change. The dividing line between the end of your original project and further improvements and enhancements can often be blurred, and a review will help to define this divide and bring to your sponsor's attention any outstanding issues.

For now though, you only need to ask some of the following questions to include in your report:

- What changes do you want to the new system?
- How can the new system be improved?
- How can the operation of the system be improved?
- What changes would you recommend to further increase the business benefit?

Presenting the review report

Keep it simple – one simple graph with key information is better than 100 tables of details. (Peter Suhr-Jessen, Project Manager, Novo Nordisk)

After you have completed all your interviews you need to review your notes and identify the main messages that emerge. In preparing your sponsor report provide a brief background to the project and its objectives from your terms of reference. Also indicate who you interviewed and their departments. Then detail the main learning points you have identified. Try to address any problem areas as well as the successes. The chances are that if you ignore something by not referring to it in your report, your sponsor will pick it up by some other means. This only makes you look devious. So be honest and deal with difficult issues up front. Most sponsors will respect your honesty and integrity.

As this type of report can be expected to be circulated to a number of other people in your organization, as well as those who contributed to the review, prepare a summary page of the key messages and results. In your presentation and covering letter to your sponsor do not forget to highlight your main achievements on the project. You must be thinking about the next project and future opportunities so make sure your sponsor is aware of your successful input.

Finally, you must indicate to your sponsor that you are seeking agreement to formally close the project on the basis that it has been satisfactorily completed. Never allow your projects to drift on endlessly. You will have other sponsors who will need your time and energy. So get written confirmation to signal the end of the project.

The main headings to include in your report are:

● Review summary
● Project background
● Project objectives
● Assessment of project manager
● Project review.

At this stage you are formally ending your consulting cycle, hopefully with a successful project result and a happy sponsor who feels positive about working with you. Thus you have laid firm foundations for your next project.

If the reviewer is pressed for time, select the appropriate interview forms from Chapter 9 and use these for gathering information from interviews.

Make sure you discuss the benefits of the review process with your sponsor at the beginning of the project and refer to the review process during the project. Sponsors hate surprises that require resource!

11 Assessing your skills

Skills needed to manage projects

Project management and golf have some similarities:
– The more you practise, the better your drive.
– Tips and tricks are mandatory for winning! (Gregoire Bouille, MIS Analyst
– Methodology and Education, Philip Morris)

This chapter will assist you in developing your effectiveness as a project manager. It is divided into two parts. Part 1 presents you with a checklist of questions concerning your project management skills, which will help you focus on the key areas. Part 2 provides you with an analysis of the skills and scope for thinking about your personal development.

Eight project management skills dimensions

There are eight skill dimensions to master in managing projects:

1 Administrator.
2 Analyst.
3 Negotiator.
4 Verbal communicator.
5 Written communicator.
6 Listener.
7 Motivator.
8 Decision-maker.

It is the combination of using all these skills at appropriate times during the cycle of a project that will make you an effective project manager.

Part 1: checklist of questions

Individually work through the following statements and tick the answer most appropriate to you. For example, if you strongly agree with a question, then place a tick against that question under the heading 'Strongly agree'. You should spend no more than ten minutes answering these questions.

Question	Strongly agree	Agree	Neither agree/nor disagree	Disagree	Strongly disagree
1 I enjoy working with and completing routine paperwork	5	4	3	2	1
2 I do not enjoy solving problems	1	2	3	4	5
3 I like dealing with people	5	4	3	2	1
4 I do not feel comfortable making presentations	1	2	3	4	5
5 I find it easy to express things in writing	5	4	3	2	1
6 I am not very patient with other people	1	2	3	4	5
7 I seem to be able to get people to do things quite easily	5	4	3	2	1
8 I do not find it easy to make quick decisions	1	2	3	4	5
9 I am not comfortable handling repetitive tasks	1	2	3	4	5
10 I can quickly get to the heart of a problem	5	4	3	2	1
11 I do not seem to be well informed or up to date with what is going on	1	2	3	4	5
12 I am very clear and concise when I speak	5	4	3	2	1
13 Other people do not find my written work persuasive	1	2	3	4	5
14 I always try to listen rather than talk	5	4	3	2	1
15 I do not seem to command respect from others	1	2	3	4	5
16 I am able to make decisions under pressure	5	4	3	2	1
17 I prefer it when things are stable rather than constantly changing	5	4	3	2	1
18 I find it difficult to understand other people's ideas very quickly	1	2	3	4	5
19 I like to influence and persuade people towards my point of view	5	4	3	2	1

Question	Strongly agree	Agree	Neither agree/nor disagree	Disagree	Strongly disagree
20 I do not use my voice tone to impact on people	1	2	3	4	5
21 I like to keep written work short and to the point	5	4	3	2	1
22 When other people are talking I do not watch their body language	1	2	3	4	5
23 I think it is important to encourage people to do things for themselves	5	4	3	2	1
24 I avoid making tough or uncomfortable decisions	1	2	3	4	5
25 I do not remain calm under pressure	1	2	3	4	5
26 I prefer to rely on logic and facts rather than intuition	5	4	3	2	1
27 I am not a good listener	1	2	3	4	5
28 I try to observe other people's body language	5	4	3	2	1
29 It takes me a lot of time to produce written material	1	2	3	4	5
30 During meetings I try to listen to peoples feelings as well as what they are saying	5	4	3	2	1
31 I think that listening to others is not important when motivating them	1	2	3	4	5
32 I do not need every piece of information to make a decision	5	4	3	2	1
33 I like organizing things and other people	5	4	3	2	1
34 I do not enjoy working with detailed information	1	2	3	4	5
35 I can be very diplomatic when the need arises	5	4	3	2	1
36 I do not like volunteering to lead a meeting or presentation	1	2	3	4	5
37 I always make detailed notes when attending meetings	5	4	3	2	1
38 I do not think about making strong eye contact when I meet people	1	2	3	4	5
39 I am always constructive when I give feedback or have to criticize someone	5	4	3	2	1
40 I try to gather all the facts and listen to people's views before making a decision	5	4	3	2	1
41 I am not always up to date with my paperwork	1	2	3	4	5
42 Having a methodology is very important to solving problems	5	4	3	2	1
43 I am not patient with people when under great pressure	1	2	3	4	5
44 I am effective in communicating my ideas	5	4	3	2	1
45 I do not find it easy to produce written material or reports	1	2	3	4	5
46 I encourage people to talk more by using open-ended questions	5	4	3	2	1
47 I do not enjoy trying to motivate people	1	2	3	4	5
48 I always try to review the effectiveness of my decisions	5	4	3	2	1

Part 2: preparing and analysing your score

Enter your score for each statement from the checklist above in the appropriate numbered box below. You will find the score in the box that you ticked for each answer. For example, if you scored 5 for question 1, then enter the number 5 in box 1 below. Then add up your scores in each row and enter the total in the box provided and then rank your scores from 1 (highest) to 8 (lowest).

						Total	*Skill area*	*Rank*
1	9	17	25	33	41		Administrator	
2	10	18	26	34	42		Analyst	
3	11	19	27	35	43		Negotiator	
4	12	20	28	36	44		Verbal communicator	
5	13	21	29	37	45		Written communicator	
6	14	22	30	38	46		Listener	
7	15	23	31	39	47		Motivator	
8	16	24	32	40	48		Decision-maker	

Score summary

Below are the eight skill dimensions to master in managing. Transfer your score from above to the following table and rank your score. This will allow you to focus on dimensions which show scope for further improvement.

Skill dimension	*Your score*	*Rank*
Administrator		
Analyst		
Negotiator		
Verbal communicator		
Written communicator		
Listener		
Motivator		
Decision-maker		

Results

For each skill area, compare your score with the bands presented below and consider the appropriate action suggested.

24 – 30	Excellent	You possess all the right skills to be effective in this area
20 – 23	Good	An effective performance score. However, you can still enhance your skills in this area
17 – 19	Moderate	Your score indicates that you need to review your skills in this area
12 – 16	Improvement needed	Your score suggest that you need to make significant improvements to your skills in this area
6 – 11	Major development need identified	Urgent action is needed for you to improve your skills in this area

Personal development: your task now

Review your score above. If there is a suggestion for further improvement, turn to the appropriate following sections in this chapter and develop your personal action plan.

This analysis is neither a performance appraisal nor definitive statement of your capability as a project manager. Use it to help you *identify areas to further develop your skills and performance* in managing projects and to *develop your own plan for action.*

Administrator

The *administrator* characteristic is defined as a set of behaviours, which involve the following:

- The accomplishment of project tasks and goals.
- A strong management of repetitive tasks and procedures.
- Adhering to routines and systematic controls.
- A focus on stability and consistency.
- Remaining calm under pressure of deadlines and work-loads.
- Effective organization skills – advising members of forthcoming meetings and outputs.
- A concern with detail and accuracy – ability to identify omissions of detail.
- Injecting urgency into projects.
- Making people constantly aware of the project's overall status.

This characteristic is needed in the following areas:

1 Preparing the Terms of Reference.
2 Managing the communications surrounding a project.
3 Organizing meetings – venues, facilities, agendas, participants.
4 Preparing meeting minutes, especially progress and review meetings.
5 Scheduling work plans of project team members.
6 Gathering and collating progress reports and recording these against the master plan.
7 Chasing project members for updates and materials.
8 Arranging travel and accommodation plans.
9 Alerting project members to problem areas.
10 Producing hard copy records of the project's progress.

Select two *of the ten items above in which you would like to improve your performance. Record this in the left-hand column below. After discussing your thoughts with a colleague, record in the right-hand column some specific actions you propose to take to improve your performance.*

I must improve my skills in:	I will:

Analyst

The *analyst* characteristic is defined as a set of behaviours involving the following:

- A strong problem-solving orientation.
- A high level of critical thinking ability.
- A reliance on fact-based decision-making processes.
- An ability to synthesize other people's thoughts and ideas.
- An interest in detail and analysis.
- Methodical work processes.
- A strategic 'big picture' outlook – the ability to 'helicopter'.
- An ability to balance short and long-term requirements.

This characteristic is needed in the following areas:

1 Preparing the project's terms of reference.
2 Preparing a breakdown of tasks.
3 Establish task dependencies.
4 Estimate a project's effort and duration.
5 Determine the project's duration using network charts.
6 Determining the critical path of tasks.
7 Allocating resources.
8 Preparing a risk analysis.
9 Preparing a contingency plan.
10 Reviewing progress against plan.
11 Replanning.

Select two of the eleven items above in which you would like to improve your performance. Record this in the left-hand column below. After discussing your thoughts with a colleague, record in the right-hand column some specific actions you propose to take to improve your performance.

I must improve my skills in:	*I will:*

ASSESSING YOUR SKILLS

Negotiator

The *negotiator* characteristic is defined as a set of behaviours involving the following:

- Confidence in influencing and persuading people.
- Flexibility in managing people relationships.
- Ability to cope with rejection.
- Determined, persistent outlook – not easily deterred from a set course of action.
- Skilled at reading other people's motives and underlying needs.
- Tough – can say 'No' without feeling guilty.
- Diplomatic at the right times.
- Willingness to challenge and confront others including senior managers and stakeholders.
- Patient and realistic in outlook.
- Emotionally controlled.

This characteristic is needed in the following areas:

1. Preparing the terms of reference
2. Persuade others to commit to or join the project team/goals
3. Harnessing resources for the project
4. Managing key project stakeholders
5. Confronting team members and stakeholders on failures to deliver
6. Negotiating new actions at project review meetings
7. Negotiating new terms when plans change

Select two *of the seven items above in which you would like to improve your performance. Record this in the left-hand column below. After discussing your thoughts with a colleague, record in the right-hand column some specific actions you propose to take to improve your performance.*

I must improve my skills in:	I will:

Verbal communicator

The *verbal communicator* characteristic is defined as a set of behaviours involving the following:

- Persuasive and articulate – ability to secure people's attention.
- Ability to present arguments succinctly and with clarity.
- Ability to communicate effectively at several levels.
- Has an effective range of verbal responses to most situations.
- Able to think on their feet.
- Varies pitch and pace of voice tone to gain maximum impact.
- Demonstrates appropriate body language.
- Displays appropriate levels of sensitivity.
- Informed and well prepared for meetings.

This characteristic is needed in the following areas:

1 Preparing the terms of reference.
2 Facilitating group/team discussions, e.g. estimating effort and duration, risk analysis.
3 Addressing the team.
4 Presenting progress at review meetings.
5 Presenting findings.
6 Acting as an intermediary between various project stakeholders.
7 Surfacing difficult or uncomfortable project issues.

Select two of the ten items above in which you would like to improve your performance. Record this in the left-hand column below. After discussing your thoughts with a colleague, record in the right-hand column some specific actions you propose to take to improve your performance.

I must improve my skills in:	I will:

Written communicator

The *written communicator* characteristic is defined as a set of behaviours involving the following:

- Capacity to present written arguments persuasively and forcefully.
- Keeps written communications brief and to the point – 'Will not use two words where one will do!'
- Ability to express complex issues with clarity.
- Extensive vocabulary which is employed with positive effect.
- Apply accuracy and precision to the written word.
- Looks for omissions.

This characteristic is needed in the following areas:

1 Preparing the terms of reference.
2 Recording notes from project meetings.
3 Communicating to team members and project stakeholders.
4 Negotiating situations.
5 Where tact and sensitivity maybe required
6 Preparing written outputs of a project plan, e.g. analysis matrix, risk and contingency.
7 Preparing progress papers and documents.
8 Assisting in formal presentations.
9 Producing draft proposals and discussion documents.
10 Producing final project reports.

Select two of the ten items above in which you would like to improve your performance. Record this in the left-hand column below. After discussing your thoughts with a colleague, record in the right-hand column some specific actions you propose to take to improve your performance.

I must improve my skills in:	I will:

Listener

The *listener* characteristic is defined as a set of behaviours involving the following:

- Willingness to ask open-ended questions.
- Willingness to listen actively.
- Patience.
- Ability to develop rapport.
- Empathy.
- Ability to absorb anger and frustration in others.
- Uses appropriate body language to mirror and reflect individual thoughts and reactions.
- Ability to interrupt and intervene at the right time.
- Gives effective feedback (nods and other non-verbal cues – eye contact).

This characteristic is needed in the following areas:

1 Preparing the terms of reference.
2 Gathering group ideas at project meetings.
3 Stimulating team discussions.
4 Managing difficult team disputes.
5 Managing one-to-one relationships.
6 Dealing with difficult people.
7 Managing stakeholder meetings.

Select two *of the seven items above in which you would like to improve your performance. Record this in the left-hand column below. After discussing your thoughts with a colleague, record in the right-hand column some specific actions you propose to take to improve your performance.*

I must improve my skills in:	I will:

Motivator

The *motivator* characteristic is defined as a set of behaviours involving the following:

- Ability to move people to action.
- Persuasive and influential.
- Commands respect from others.
- Is consistent in people management practices.
- Able to get more out of people.
- Able to enthuse and excite people.
- Attracts people.
- Highly developed interpersonal skills.
- Achieves results through others rather than self – but also leads by example.
- Ability to provide constructive criticism and positive alternatives.

This characteristic is needed in the following areas:

1 Preparing the terms of reference.
2 Motivating team members to 'buy into the project'.
3 Motivating team members to complete their work and tasks.
4 Giving advice and guidance when needed.
5 Moments of poor progress, low morale or major setbacks.
6 Participating in team activities such as estimating effort, preparing plans.
7 Encouraging participants to higher levels of performance.
8 Persuading supporters and stakeholders.

Select two of the eight items above in which you would like to improve your performance. Record this in the left-hand column below. After discussing your thoughts with a colleague, record in the right-hand column some specific actions you propose to take to improve your performance.

I must improve my skills in:	I will:

Decision-maker

The *decision-maker* characteristic is defined as a set of behaviours involving the following:

- An action orientation.
- Capacity to be decisive when dealing with incomplete information.
- Ability to absorb lots of information and distil it into essential elements.
- Logical.
- Non-emotional.
- Ability to stay focused on the 'big picture'.
- Does not mind upsetting people if the final goal demands it.
- Absorbs essential viewpoints before committing to action.
- Has courage and conviction in their decision-making ability.

This characteristic is needed in the following areas:

1 Agreeing the terms of reference with the sponsor.
2 Making decisions with TOR changes.
3 Deciding on the uses of project resources.
4 Resolving conflicts between team members or stakeholders.
5 Prioritizing tasks in the face of competing demands.

Select two of the five items above in which you would like to improve your performance. Record this in the left-hand column below. After discussing your thoughts with a colleague, record in the right-hand column some specific actions you propose to take to improve your performance.

I must improve my skills in:	*I will:*

Further reading

Belbin, R. M. (1985) *Managing Teams*. Butterworth-Heinemann.

Blanchard, K. and Johnson, S. (1985) *The One Minute Manager*. Fontana.

de Bono, E. (1973) *Lateral Thinking*. Harper and Row.

Buzan, T. (1983) *Use Both Sides of your Brain*. E. P. Dutton.

CCTA, *PRINCE – an Outline*, HMSO.

Clelland, D. and King, W. (1968) *Systems Analysis and Project Management*. McGraw-Hill.

Cooper, D. F. and Chapman, C. (1987) *Risk Analysis for Larger Projects*. Wiley.

Davies, D. (1985) New Projects: Beware of False Economies. *Harvard Business Review*, March–April.

Drucker, P. F. (1988) The Coming of the New Organization. *Harvard Business Review*. January–February.

Garvin, D. A. (1987) Competing on the Eight Dimensions of Quality. *Harvard Business Review*, November–December.

Harrison, F. L. (1985) *Advances in Project Management*. Gower.

Haynes, M. E. (1990) *Project Management: From Idea to Implementation*. Kogan Page.

Hersey, P. and Blanchard, K. H. (1988) *Situational Leadership, Management of Organizational Behavior: Utilizing Human Resource*. 5th edn, Prentice Hall.

Kanter, R. M. (1983) *The Change Masters*. Simon and Schuster.

Kanter, R. M. (1989) The New Managerial Work. *Harvard Business Review*, November–December.

Kerzner, H. (1984) *Project Management: A Systems Approach to Planning, Scheduling and Controlling*. Van Nostrand Reinhold.

Leon, R. O. (1971) *Manage More by Doing Less*. McGraw-Hill.

Lock, D. (1989) *Project Management*. Gower.

Lockyear, K. and Gordon, J. (1991) *Critical Path Analysis and Other Project Network Techniques*. Pitman.

Martin, C. (1976) *Project Management: How to Make it Work*. AMACOM (A division of the American Management Association).

Maslow, A. (1970) *Motivation and Personality*. Harper and Row.

Miller, R. W. (1962) How to Plan and Control with PERT. *Harvard Business Review*, **40** (2), March–April, 93–104.

Myers, M. S. (1964) Who Are your Motivated Workers? *Harvard Business Review*, January–February.

Peters, T. (1987) *Thriving on Chaos*. Alfred A. Knopf.

Peters, T. and Waterman, R. H. (1982) *In Search of Excellence: Lessons from America's Best Run Companies*. Harper and Row.

Schroder, H. (1970) Making Project Management Work. *Management Review*, December, 24–8.

Steiner, G. and William, R. (1986) *Industrial Project Management*. Macmillan.

Taylor, W. J. and Watling, T. F. (1970) *Successful Project Management*. Business Books.

Thomas, M. and Elbeik, S. (1996) *Supercharge your Management Role: Making the Transition to Internal Consultant*. Butterworth-Heinemann.

Webb A. (1994) *Managing Innovative Projects*. Chapman and Hall.

Index

Project Director: Software to help you manage your projects

Welcome to *project DIRECTOR*™, a powerful software application that takes its roots from many of the techniques described in this book.

It really allows you to manage multiple projects, by offering you a comprehensive, yet simple set of essential project tools and is now available for you to try.

With *project DIRECTOR*™ you can:

- ☑ Define your objectives, scope and business benefit
- ☑ Note down any constraints and assumptions you are making
- ☑ Enter deliverables
- ☑ Estimate the work that is needed to complete a deliverable
- ☑ Allocate people to deliverables
- ☑ Measure the risk and prepare contingencies
- ☑ Record your sponsor's detailed requirements (really understand their needs)
- ☑ Use time sheets to record actual time spent on deliverables
- ☑ Print a variety of essential project reports
- ☑ Work on a single PC or use your local network and connect your entire team
- ☑ Define users, passwords and restrict access given to others
- ☑ Purchase the Microsoft® Access® code and customise it to your needs

System Requirements

- Windows® 3.x, Windows® 95, Windows® 98 or NT Workstation 4.0 or higher

- 486 processor, Pentium® or Pentium® II processor

- 12MB or more of RAM available to *project DIRECTOR*™

- 20MB or more of available hard disk space

- CD-ROM drive for installation

Contact IT Centre now for your evaluation copy

Please contact IT Centre by email at info@itcentre.com for your evaluation copy of *project DIRECTOR*™. Alternatively you can visit their web site at www.itcentre.com for more information.